# THE IMAGINARY MARRIAGE

## HENRY ST. JOHN COOPER

1st WORLD
LIBRARY
Literary Society

# The Imaginary Marriage

### Henry St. John Cooper

© 1st World Library, 2008
PO Box 2211
Fairfield, IA 52556
www.1stworldlibrary.com
First Edition

LCCN: 2007935385

Softcover ISBN: 978-1-4218-9338-9
Hardcover ISBN: 978-1-4218-9438-6
eBook ISBN: 978-1-4218-9238-2

Purchase *"The Imaginary Marriage"*
as a traditional bound book at:
www.1stWorldLibrary.com/purchase.asp?ISBN=978-1-4218-9338-9

1st World Library is a literary, educational organization
dedicated to:

- Creating a free internet library of downloadable ebooks

- Hosting writing competitions and offering book publishing scholarships.

# 1ˢᵗ World Library Literary Society

## Giving Back to the World

"If you want to work on the core problem, it's early school literacy."

**- James Barksdale, former CEO of Netscape**

"No skill is more crucial to the future of a child, or to a democratic and prosperous society, than literacy."

**- Los Angeles Times**

"Literacy... means far more than learning how to read and write... The aim is to transmit... knowledge and promote social participation."

**- UNESCO**

"Literacy is not a luxury, it is a right and a responsibility. If our world is to meet the challenges of the twenty-first century we must harness the energy and creativity of all our citizens."

**- President Bill Clinton**

"Parents should be encouraged to read to their children, and teachers should be equipped with all available techniques for teaching literacy, so the varying needs and capacities of individual kids can be taken into account."

**- Hugh Mackay**

# CHAPTER I

## A MASTERFUL WOMAN

"Don't talk to me, miss," said her ladyship. "I don't want to hear any nonsense from you!"

The pretty, frightened girl who shared the drawing-room at this moment with Lady Linden of Cornbridge Manor House had not dared to open her lips. But that was her ladyship's way, and "Don't talk to me!" was a stock expression of hers. Few people were permitted to talk in her ladyship's presence. In Cornbridge they spoke of her with bated breath as a "rare masterful woman," and they had good cause.

Masterful and domineering was Lady Linden of Cornbridge, yet she was kind-hearted, though she tried to disguise the fact.

In Cornbridge she reigned supreme, men and women trembled at her approach. She penetrated the homes of the cottagers, she tasted of their foods, she rated them on uncleanliness, drunkenness, and thriftlessness; she lectured them on cooking.

On many a Saturday night she raided, single-handed, the Plough Inn and drove forth the sheepish revellers, personally conducting them to their homes and wives.

They respected her in Cornbridge as the reigning sovereign of her small estate, and none did she rule more autocratically and completely than her little nineteen-year-old niece Marjorie.

A pretty, timid, little maid was Marjorie, with soft yellow hair, a sweet oval face, with large pathetic blue eyes and a timid, uncertain little rosebud of a mouth.

"A rare sweet maid her be," they said of her in the village, "but terribul tim'rous, and I lay her ladyship du give she a rare time of it...." Which was true.

"Don't talk to me, miss!" her ladyship said to the silent girl. "I know what is best for you; and I know, too, what you don't think I know—ha, ha!" Her ladyship laughed terribly. "I know that you have been meeting that worthless young scamp, Tom Arundel!"

"Oh, aunt, he is not worthless—"

"Financially he isn't worth a sou—and that's what I mean, and don't interrupt. I am your guardian, you are entirely in my charge, and until you arrive at the age of twenty-five I can withhold your fortune from you if you marry in opposition to me and my wishes. But you won't—you won't do anything of the kind. You will marry the man I select for you, the man I have already selected—what did you say, miss?

"And now, not another word. Hugh Alston is the man I have selected for you. He is in love with you, there isn't a finer lad living. He has eight thousand a year, and Hurst Dormer is one of the best old properties in Sussex. So that's quite

Henry St. John Cooper

enough, and I don't want to hear any more nonsense about Tom Arundel. I say nothing against him personally. Colonel Arundel is a gentleman, of course, otherwise I would not permit you to know his son; but the Arundels haven't a pennypiece to fly with and—and now—Now I see Hugh coming up the drive. Leave me. I want to talk to him. Go into the garden, and wait by the lily-pond. In all probability Hugh will have something to say to you before long."

"Oh, aunt, I—"

"Shut up!" said her ladyship briefly.

Marjorie went out, with hanging head and bursting heart. She believed herself the most unhappy girl in England. She loved; who could help loving happy-go-lucky, handsome Tom Arundel, who well-nigh worshipped the ground her little feet trod upon? It was the first love and the only love of her life, and of nights she lay awake picturing his bright, young boyish face, hearing again all the things he had said to her till her heart was well-nigh bursting with love and longing for him.

But she did not hate Hugh. Who could hate Hugh Alston, with his cheery smile, his ringing voice, his big generous heart, and his fine manliness? Not she! But from the depths of her heart she wished Hugh Alston a great distance away from Cornbridge.

"Hello, Hugh!" said her ladyship. He had come in, a man of two-and-thirty, big and broad, with suntanned face and eyes as blue as the tear-dimmed eyes of the girl who had gone miserably down to the lily-pond.

Fair haired was Hugh, ruddy of cheek, with no particular beauty to boast of, save the wholesomeness and cleanliness of his young manhood. He seemed to bring into the room a scent of the open country, of the good brown earth and of the clean wind of heaven.

"Hello, Hugh!" said Lady Linden.

"Hello, my lady," said he, and kissed her. It had been his habit from boyhood, also it had been his lifelong habit to love and respect the old dame, and to feel not the slightest fear of her. In this he was singular, and because he was the one person who did not fear her she preferred him to anyone else.

"Hugh," she said—she went straight to the point, she always did; as a hunter goes at a hedge, so her ladyship without prevarication went at the matter she had in hand—"I have been talking to Marjorie about Tom Arundel—"

His cheery face grew a little grave.

"Yes?"

"Well, it is absurd—you realise that?"

"I suppose so, but—" He paused.

"It is childish folly!"

"Do you think so? Do you think that she—" Again he paused, with a nervousness and diffidence usually foreign to him.

"She's only a gel," said her ladyship. Her ladyship was Sussex born, and talked Sussex when she became excited. "She's only a gel, and gels have their fancies. I had my own—but bless you, they don't last. She don't know her own mind."

Henry St. John Cooper

"He's a good fellow," said Hugh generously.

"A nice lad, but he won't suit me for Marjorie's husband. Hugh, the gel's in the garden, she is sitting by the lily-pond and believes her heart is broken, but it isn't! Go and prove it isn't; go now!"

He met her eyes and flushed red. "I'll go and have a talk to Marjorie," he said. "You haven't been—too rough with her, have you?"

"Rough! I know how to deal with gels. I told her that I had the command of her money, her four hundred a year till she was twenty-five, and not a bob of it should she touch if she married against my wish. Now go and talk to her—and talk sense—" She paused. "You know what I mean—sense!"

A very pretty picture, the slender white-clad, drooping figure with its crown of golden hair made, sitting on the bench beside the lily-pond. Her hands were clasped, her eyes fixed on the stagnant green water over which the dragon-flies skimmed.

Coming across the soundless turf, he stood for a moment to look at her.

Hurst Dormer was a fine old place, yet of late to him it had grown singularly dull and cheerless. He had loved it all his life, but latterly he had realised that there was something missing, something without which the old house could not be home to him, and in his dreams waking and sleeping he had seen this same little white-clad figure seated at the foot of the great table in the dining-hall.

He had seen her in his mind's eye doing those little housewifely duties that the mistresses of Hurst Dormer had always loved to do, her slender fingers busy with the rare and delicate old china, or the lavender-scented linen, or else in the wonderful old garden, the gracious little mistress of all and of his heart.

And now she sat drooping like a wilted lily beside the green pond, because of her love for another man, and his honest heart ached that it should be so.

"Marjorie!" he said.

She lifted a tear-stained face and held out her hand' to him silently.

He patted her hand gently, as one pats the hand of a child. "Is—is it so bad, little girl? Do you care for him so much?"

"Better than my life!" she said. "Oh, if you knew!"

"I see," he said quietly. He sat staring at the green waters, stirred now and again by the fin of a lazy carp. He realised that there would be no sweet girlish, golden-haired little mistress for Hurst Dormer, and the realisation hurt him badly.

The girl seemed to have crept a little closer to him, as for comfort and protection.

"She has made up her mind, and nothing will change it. She wants you to—to marry me. She's told me so a hundred times. She won't listen to anything else; she says you—you care for me, Hugh."

"Supposing I care so much, little girl, that I want your happiness above everything in this world. Supposing—I clear out?" he said—"clear right away, go to Africa, or somewhere or other?"

"She would make me wait till you came back, and you'd have to come back, Hugh, because there is always Hurst Dormer. There's no way out for me, none. If only—only you were married; that is the only thing that would have saved me!"

"But I'm not!"

She sighed. "If only you were, if only you could say to her, 'I can't ask Marjorie to marry me, because I am already married!' It sounds rubbish, doesn't it, Hugh; but if it were only true!"

"Supposing—I did say it?"

"Oh, Hugh, but—" She looked up at him quickly. "But it would be a lie!"

"I know, but lies aren't always the awful things they are supposed to be—if one told a lie to help a friend, for instance, such a lie might be forgiven, eh?"

"But—" She was trembling; she looked eagerly into his eyes, into her cheeks had come a flush, into her eyes the brightness of a new, though as yet vague, hope. "It—it sounds so impossible!"

"Nothing is actually impossible. Listen, little maid. She sent me here to you to talk sense, as she put it. That meant she sent me here to ask you to marry me, and I meant to do it. I think perhaps you know why"—he lifted her hand to his lips and kissed it—"but I shan't now, I never shall. Little girl, we're going to be what we've always been, the best and truest of friends, and I've got to find a way to help you and Tom—"

"Hugh, if you told her that you were married, and not free, she wouldn't give another thought to opposing Tom and me—it is only because she wants me to marry you that she opposes Tom! Oh, Hugh, if—if—if you could, if it were possible!" She was trembling with excitement, and the sweet colour was coming and going in her cheeks.

"Supposing I did it?" he said, and spoke his thoughts aloud. "Of course it would be a shock to her, perhaps she wouldn't believe!"

"She would believe anything you said..."

"It is rather a rotten thing to do," he thought, "yet...." He looked at the bright, eager face, it would make her happy; he knew that what she said was true—Lady Linden would not oppose Tom Arundel if marriage between Marjorie and himself was out of the question. It would be making the way clear for her: it would be giving her happiness, doing her the greatest service that he could. Of his own sacrifice, his own disappointment he thought not now; realisation of that would come later.

At first it seemed to him a mad, a nonsensical scheme, yet it was one that might so easily be carried out. If one doubt was left as to whether he would do it, it was gone the next moment.

"Hugh, would you do—would you do this for me?"

"There is very little that I wouldn't do for you, little maid," he said, "and if I can help you to your happiness I am going to do it."

She crept closer to him; she laid her cheek against his shoulder, and held his hand in hers.

Henry St. John Cooper

"Tell me just what you will say."

"I haven't thought that out yet."

"But you must."

"I know. You see, if I say I am married, naturally she will ask me a few questions."

"When she gets—gets her breath!" Marjorie said with a laugh; it was the first time she had laughed, and he liked to hear it.

"The first will probably be, How long have I been married?"

"Do you remember you used to come to Marlbury to see me when I was at school at Miss Skinner's?"

"Rather!"

"That was three years ago. Supposing you married about then?"

"Fine," Hugh said. "I married three years ago. What month?"

"June," she said; "it's a lovely month!"

"I was married in June, nineteen hundred and eighteen, my lady," said Hugh. "Where at, though?"

"Why, Marlbury, of course!"

"Of course! Splendid place to get married in, delightful romantic old town!"

"It is a hateful place, but that doesn't matter," said Marjorie.

She seemed to snuggle up a little closer to him, her lips were rippling with smiles, her bright eyes saw freedom and love, her heart was very warm with gratitude to this man who was helping her. But she could not guess, how could she, how in spite of the laughter on his lips there was a great ache and a feeling of emptiness at his heart.

"So now we have it all complete," he said. "I was married in June, nineteen eighteen at Marlbury; my wife and I did not get on, we parted. She had a temper, so had I, a most unhappy affair, and there you are!" He laughed.

"All save one thing," Marjorie said.

"Goodness, what have I forgotten?"

"Only the lady's name."

"You are right. She must have a name of course, something nice and romantic—Gladys something, eh?"

Marjorie shook her head.

"Clementine," suggested Hugh. "No, won't do, eh? Now you put your thinking cap on and invent a name, something romantic and pretty. Let's hear from you, Marjorie."

"Do you like—Joan Meredyth?" she said.

"Splendid! What a clever little brain!" He shut his eyes. "I married Miss Joan Meredyth on the first of June, or was it the second, in the year nineteen hundred and eighteen? We lived a cat-and-dog existence, and parted with mutual recriminations, since when I have not seen her! Marjorie, do you think she will swallow it?"

"If you tell her; but, Hugh, will you—will you?"

"Little girl, is it going to help you?"

"You know it is!" she whispered.

"Then I shall tell her!"

Marjorie lifted a pair of soft arms and put them about his neck.

"Hugh!" she said, "Hugh, if—if I had never known Tom, I—"

"I know," he said. "I know. God bless you." He stooped and kissed her on the cheek, and rose.

It was a mad thing this that he was to do, yet he never considered its madness, its folly. It would help her, and Hurst Dormer would never know its golden-haired mistress, after all.

## CHAPTER II

## IN WHICH HUGH BREAKS THE NEWS

Lady Linden had just come in from one of her usual and numerous inspections, during which she had found it necessary to reprove one of the under-gardeners. She had described him to himself, his character, his appearance and his methods from her own point of view, and had left the man stupefied and amazed at the extent of her vocabulary and her facility of expression. He was still scratching his head, dazedly, when she came into the drawing-room.

"Hugh, you here? Where is Marjorie?"

"Down by the pond, I think," he said, with an attempt at airiness.

"In a moment you will make me angry. You know what I wish to know. Did you propose to Marjorie, Hugh?"

"Did I—" He seemed astonished. "Did I what?"

"Propose to Marjorie! Good heavens, man, isn't that why I sent you there?"

"I certainly did not propose to her. How on earth could I?"

Henry St. John Cooper

"There is no reason on earth why you should not have proposed to her that I can see."

"But there is one that I can see." He paused. "A man can't invite a young woman to marry him—when he is already married!"

It was out! He scarcely dared to look at her. Lady Linden said nothing; she sat down.

"Hugh!" She had found breath and words at last. "Hugh Alston! Did I hear you aright?"

"I believe you did!"

"You mean to tell me that you—you are a married man?"

He nodded. He realised that he was not a good liar.

"I would like some particulars," she said coldly. "Hugh Alston, I should be very interested to know where she is!"

"I don't know!"

"You are mad. When were you married?"

"June nineteen eighteen," he said glibly.

"Where?"

"At Marlbury!"

"Good gracious! That is where Marjorie used to go to school!"

"Yes, it was when I went down to see her there, and—"

"You met this woman you married? And her name?"

"Joan," he said—"Joan Meredyth!"

"Joan—Meredyth!" said Lady Linden. She closed her eyes; she leaned back in her chair. "That girl!"

A chill feeling of alarm swept over him. She spoke, her ladyship spoke, as though such a girl existed, as though she knew her personally. And the name was a pure invention! Marjorie had invented it—at least, he believed so.

"You—you don't know her?"

"Know her—of course I know her. Didn't Marjorie bring her here from Miss Skinner's two holidays running? A very beautiful and brilliant girl, the loveliest girl I think I ever saw! Really, Hugh Alston, though I am surprised and pained at your silence and duplicity, I must absolve you. I always regarded you as more or less a fool, but Joan Meredyth is a girl any man might fall in love with!"

Hugh sat gripping the arms of his chair. What had he done, or rather what had Marjorie done? What desperate muddle had that little maid led him into? He had counted on the name being a pure invention, and now—

"Where is she?" demanded Lady Linden.

"I don't know—we—we parted!"

"Why?"

"We didn't get on, you see. She'd got a temper, and so—"

"Of course she had a temper. She is a spirited gel, full of life and fire and intelligence. I wouldn't give twopence for a woman without a temper—certainly she had a temper! Bah, don't talk to me, sir—you sit there and tell me you were content to let her go, let a beautiful creature like that go merely because she had a temper?"

"She—she went. I didn't let her go; she just went!"

"Yes," Lady Linden said thoughtfully, "I suppose she did. It is just what Joan would do! She saw that she was not appreciated; you wrangled, or some folly, and she simply went. She would—so would I have gone! And now, where is she?"

"I tell you I don't know!"

"You've never sought her?"

"Never! I—I—now look here," he went on, "don't take it to heart too much. She is quite all right—that is, I expect—"

"You expect!" she said witheringly. "Here you sit; you have a beautiful young wife, the most brilliant girl I ever met, and—and you let her go! Don't talk to me!"

"No, I won't; let's drop it! We will discuss it some other time—it is a matter I prefer not to talk about! Naturally it is rather—painful to me!"

"So I should think!"

"Yes, I much prefer not to talk about it. Let's discuss Marjorie!"

"Confound Marjorie!"

"Marjorie is the sweetest little soul in the world, and—"

"It's a pity you didn't think of that three years ago!"

"And Tom Arundel is a fine fellow; no one can say one word against him!"

"I don't wish to discuss them! If Marjorie is obsessed with this folly about young Arundel, it will be her misfortune. If she wants to marry him she will probably regret it. I intended her to marry you; but since it can't be, I don't feel any particular interest in the matter of Marjorie's marriage at the moment! Now tell me about Joan at once!"

"Believe me, I—I much prefer not to: it is a sore subject, a matter I never speak about!"

"Oh, go away then—and leave me to myself. Let me think it all out!"

He went gladly enough; he made his way back to the lily-pond.

"Marjorie," he said tragically, "what have you done?"

"Oh, Hugh!" She was trembling at once.

"No, no, dear, don't worry; it is nothing. She believes every word, and I feel sure it will be all right for you and Tom, but, oh Marjorie—that name, I thought you had invented it!"

Marjorie flushed. "It was the name of a girl at Miss Skinner's: she was a great, great friend of mine. She was two years older than I, and just as sweet and beautiful as her name, and when you were casting about for one I—I just thought of it, Hugh. It hasn't done any harm, has it?"

Henry St. John Cooper

"I hope not, only, don't you see, you've made me claim an existing young lady as my wife, and if she turned up some time or other—"

"But she won't! When she left school she went out to Australia to join her uncle there, and she will in all probability never come back to England."

Hugh drew a sigh of relief. "That's all right then! It's all right, little girl; it is all right. I believe things are going to be brighter for you now."

"Thanks to you, Hugh!"

"You know there is nothing in this world—" He looked down at the lovely face, alive with gratitude and happiness. His dreams were ended, the "might-have-been" would never be, but he knew that there was peace in that little breast at last.

# CHAPTER III

## JOAN MEREDYTH, TYPIST

Mr. Philip Slotman touched the electric buzzer on his desk and then watched the door. He was an unpleasant—looking man, strangely corpulent as to body, considering his face was cast in lean and narrow mould, the nose large, prominent and hooked, the lips full, fleshy, and of cherry—like redness, the eyes small, mean, close together and deep set. The over—corpulent body was attired lavishly. It was dressed in a fancy waistcoat, a morning coat, elegantly striped trousers of lavender hue and small pointed—toed, patent—leather boots, with bright tan uppers. The rich aroma of an expensive cigar hung about the atmosphere of Mr. Slotman's office. This and his clothes, and the large diamond ring that twinkled on his finger, proclaimed him a person of opulence.

The door opened and a girl came in; she carried a notebook and her head very high. She trod like a young queen, and in spite of the poor black serge dress she wore, there was much of regal dignity about her. Dark brown hair that waved back from a broad and low forehead, a pair of lustrous eyes filled now with contempt and aversion, eyes shielded by lashes that, when she slept, lay like a silken fringe upon her cheeks. Her nose was redeemed from the purely classical by the merest suggestion of tip-tiltedness, that gave humour, expression and tenderness to the whole face—tenderness and sweetness that with strength was further betrayed by the finely cut, red-lipped mouth and the strong little chin, carried so proudly on the white column of her neck.

Her figure was that of a young goddess, and a goddess she looked as she swept disdainfully into Mr. Philip Slotman's office, shorthand notebook in her hand.

"I want you to take a letter to Jarvis and Purcell, Miss Meredyth," he said. "Please sit down. Er—hum—'Dear Sirs, With regard to your last communication received on the fourteenth instant, I beg—'"

Mr. Slotman moved, apparently negligently, from his leather-covered armchair. He rose, he sauntered around the desk, then suddenly he flung off all pretence at lethargy, and with a quick step put himself between the girl and the door.

"Now, my dear," he said, "you've got to listen to me!"

"I am listening to you." She turned contemptuous grey eyes on him.

"Hang the letter! I don't mean that. You've got to listen about other things!"

He stretched out his hand to touch her, and she drew back. She rose, and her eyes flashed.

"If you touch me, Mr. Slotman, I shall—" She paused; she looked about her; she picked up a heavy ebony ruler from his desk. "I shall defend myself!"

"Don't be a fool," he said, yet took a step backwards, for there was danger in her eyes.

"Look here, you won't get another job in a hurry, and you know it. Shorthand typists are not wanted these days, the schools are turning out thousands of 'em, all more or less bad; but I—I ain't talking about that, dear—" He took a step towards her, and then recoiled, seeing her knuckles shine whitely as she gripped the ruler. "Come, be sensible!"

"Are you going to persist in this annoyance of me?" she demanded. "Can't I make you understand that I am here to do my work and for no other purpose?"

"Supposing," he said, "supposing—I—I asked you to marry me?"

He had never meant to say this, yet he had said it, for the fascination of her was on him.

"Supposing you did? Do you think I would consent to marry such a man as you?" She held her head very proudly.

"Do you mean that you would refuse?"

"Of course!"

He seemed staggered; he looked about him as one amazed. He had kept this back as the last, the supreme temptation, the very last card in his hand; and he had played it, and behold, it proved to be no trump.

"I would neither marry you nor go out with you, nor do I wish to have anything to say to you, except so far as business is concerned. As that seems impossible, it will be better for me to give you a week's notice, Mr. Slotman."

"You'll be sorry for it," he said—"infernally sorry for it. It ain't pleasant to starve, my girl!"

"I had to do it, I had to, or I could not have respected myself any longer," the girl thought, as she made her way home that evening to the boarding-house, where for two pounds a week she was fed and lodged. But to be workless! It had been the nightmare of her dreams, the haunting fear of her waking hours.

In her room at the back of the house, to which the jingle of the boarding-house piano could yet penetrate, she sat for a time in deep thought. The past had held a few friends, folk who had been kind to her. Pride had held her back; she had never asked help of any of them. She thought of the Australian uncle who had invited her to come out to him when she should leave school, and then had for some reason changed his mind and sent her a banknote for a hundred pounds instead. She had felt glad and relieved at the time, but now she regretted his decision. Yet there had been a few friends; she wrote down the names as they occurred to her.

There was old General Bartholomew, who had known her father. There was Mrs. Ransome. No, she believed now that she had heard that Mrs. Ransome was dead; perhaps the General too, yet she would risk it. There was Lady Linden, Marjorie Linden's aunt. She knew but little of her, but remembered her as at heart a kindly, though an autocratic dame. She remembered, too, that one of Lady Linden's hobbies had been to establish Working Guilds and Rural Industries, Village Crafts, and suchlike in her village. In connection with some of these there might be work for her.

She wrote to all that she could think of, a letter of which she made six facsimile copies. It was not a begging appeal, but a dignified little reminder of her existence.

"If you could assist me to obtain any work by which I might live, you would be putting me under a deep debt of gratitude," she wrote.

Before she slept that night all six letters were in the post. She wished them good luck one by one as she dropped them into the letter-box, the six sprats that had been flung into the sea of fortune. Would one of them catch for her a mackerel? She wondered.

"You'd best take back that notice," Slotman said to her the next morning. "You won't find it so precious easy to find a job, my girl; and, after all, what have I done?"

"Annoyed me, insulted me ever since I came here," she said quietly. "And of course I shall not stay!"

"Insulted you! Is it an insult to ask you to be my wife?"

"It seems so to me," she said quietly. "If you had meant that—at first—it would have been different; now it is only an insult!"

Three days passed, and there came answers. She had been right, Mrs. Ransome was dead, and there was no one who could do anything for Miss Meredyth.

General Bartholomew was at Harrogate, and her letter had been sent on to him there, wrote a polite secretary. And then there came a letter that warmed the girl's heart and brought back all her belief and faith in human nature.

"MY DEAREST CHILD,

"Your letter came as a welcome surprise—to think that you are looking for employment! Well, we must see to this—I promise you, you will not have far to look. Come here to me at once, and be sure that everything will be put right and all misunderstandings wiped out. I am keeping your letter a secret from everyone, even from Marjorie, that your coming shall be the more unexpected, and the greater surprise and pleasure. But come without delay, and believe me to be,

"Your very affectionate friend,
"HARRIET LINDEN."

"P.S.—I suggest that you wire me the day and the train, so that I can meet you. Don't lose any time, and be sure that all past unhappiness can be ended, and the future faced with the certainty of brighter and happier days."

Over this letter Joan Meredyth pondered a great deal. It was a warm-hearted and affectionate response to her somewhat stilted little appeal. Yet what did the old lady mean, to what did the veiled reference apply?

"So you mean going, then?" Slotman asked.

"I told you I would go, and I shall. I leave to-morrow."

"You'll be glad to come back," he said. He looked at her, and there was eagerness in his eyes. "Joan, don't be a fool, stay. I could give you a good time, and—"

But she had turned her back on him.

She had written to Lady Linden thanking her for her kindly letter.

"I shall come to you on Saturday for the week-end, if I may. I find there is a train at a quarter-past three. I shall come by that to Cornbridge Station.

"Believe me,
"Yours gratefully and affectionately,
"JOAN MEREDYTH."

There was a subdued excitement about Lady Linden during the Thursday and the Friday, and an irritating air of secretiveness.

"Foolish, foolish young people! Both so good and so worthy in their way—the girl beautiful and clever, the man as fine and honest and upright a young fellow as ever trod this earth—donkeys! Perhaps they can't be driven—very often donkeys can't; but they can be led!"

To Hugh Alston, at Hurst Dormer, seven miles away, Lady Linden had written.

"MY DEAR HUGH,

"I want you to come here Saturday; it is a matter of vital importance." (She had a habit of underlining her words to give them emphasis, and she underscored "vital" three times.) "I want you to time your arrival for half-past five, a nice time for tea. Don't be earlier, and don't be later. And, above all, don't fail me, or I will never forgive you."

"I expect," Hugh thought, "that she is going to make a public announcement of the engagement between Marjorie and Tom Arundel."

It was precisely at half-past five that Hugh stepped out of his two-seater car and demanded admittance at the door of the Manor House.

"Oh, Mr. Alston," the footman said, "my lady is expecting you. She told me to show you straight into the drawing-room, and she and—" The man paused.

"Her ladyship will be with you in a few moments, sir."

"There is festival in the air here, Perkins, and mystery and secrecy too, eh?"

"Yes, sir, thank you, sir," the man said. "This way, Mr. Alston."

And now in the drawing-room Hugh was cooling his heels.

Why this mystery? Where was Marjorie? Why didn't his aunt come?

Then someone came, the door opened. Into the room stepped a tall girl—a girl with the most beautiful face he thought he had ever seen in his life. She looked at him calmly and casually, and seemed to hesitate; and then behind her appeared Lady Linden, flushed, and evidently agitated.

"There," she said, "there, my dears—I have brought you together again, and now everything must be made quite all right! Joan, darling, here is your husband! Go to him, forgive him if there is aught to forgive. Ask forgiveness, child, in your turn, and then—then kiss and be friends, as husband and wife should be."

She beamed on them both, then swiftly retreated, and the door behind Joan Meredyth quickly closed.

## CHAPTER IV

## FACE TO FACE

It was, Hugh Alston decided, the most beautiful face he had ever seen in his life and the coldest, or so it seemed to him. She was looking at him with cool questioning in her grey eyes, her lips drawn to a hard line.

He saw her as she stood before him, and as he saw her now, so would he carry the memory of the picture she made in his mind for many a day to come—tall, perhaps a little taller than the average woman, tall by comparison with Marjorie Linden, brown of hair and grey of eye, with a disdainfully enquiring look about her.

He was not a man who usually noticed a woman's clothes, yet the picture impressed on his mind of this girl was a very complete one. She was wearing a dress that instinct told him was of some cheap material. She might have bought it ready-made, she might have made it herself, or some unskilled dressmaker might have turned it out cheaply. Poverty was the note it struck, her boots were small and neat, well-worn. Yes, poverty was the keynote to it all.

It was she, womanlike, who broke the silence.

Henry St. John Cooper

"Well? I am waiting for some explanation of all the extraordinary things that have been said to me since I have been in this house. You, of course, heard what Lady Linden said as she left us?"

"I heard," he said. His cheeks turned red. Was ever a man in a worse position? The questioning grey eyes stared at him so coldly that he lost his head. He wanted to apologise, to explain, yet he knew that he could not explain. It was Marjorie who had brought him into this, but he must respect the girl's secret, on which so much depended for her.

"Please answer me," Joan Meredyth said. "You heard Lady Linden advise us, you and myself, to make up a quarrel that has never taken place; you heard her—" She paused, a great flush suddenly stole over her face, adding enormously to her attractiveness, but quickly as it came, it went.

What could he say? Vainly he racked his brains. He must say something, or the girl would believe him to be fool as well as knave. Ideas, excuses, lies entered his mind, he put them aside instantly, as being unworthy of him and of her, yet he must tell her—something.

"When—when I used your name, believe me, I had no idea that it was the property of a living woman—"

"When you used my name? I don't understand you!"

"I claimed that I was married to a Miss Joan Meredyth—"

"I still don't understand you. You say you claimed that you were married—are you married to anyone?"

"No!"

"Then—then—" Again the glorious flush came into her cheeks, but was gone again, leaving her whiter, colder than before, only her eyes seemed to burn with the fire of anger and contempt.

"I am beginning to understand, for some reason of your own, you used my name, you informed Lady Linden that you—and I were—married?"

"Yes," he said.

"And it was, of course, a vile lie, an insolent lie!" Her voice quivered. "It has subjected me to humiliation and annoyance. I do not think that a girl has ever been placed in such a false position as I have been through your—cowardly lie."

He had probably never known actual fear in his life, nor a sense of shame such as he knew now. He had nothing to say, he wanted to explain, yet could not, for Marjorie's sake. If Lady Linden knew how she had been deceived, she would naturally be furiously angry, and the brunt of her anger would fall on Marjorie, and this must not be.

So, silent, unable to speak a word in self-defence, he stood listening, shame-faced, while the girl spoke. Every word she uttered was cutting and cruel, yet she shewed no temper. He could have borne with that.

"You probably knew of me, and knew that I was alone in the world with no one to champion me. You knew that I was poor, Mr. Alston, and so a fit butt for your cowardly jest. My poverty has brought me into contact with strange people, cads; but the worst, the cruellest, the lowest of all is yourself! I had hoped to have found rest and refuge here for a little time, but you have driven me out. Oh, I did not believe that anything so despicable, so unmanly as you could exist. I do not know why you have done this, perhaps it is your idea of humour."

"Believe me—" he stammered, yet could say no more; and then a sense of anger, of outraged honesty, came to him. Of course he had been foolish, yet he had been misled. To hear this girl speak, one would think that he had deliberately set to work to annoy and insult her, she of whose existence he had not even known.

"My poverty," she said, and flung her head back as she spoke, "has made me the butt, the object for the insolence and insult of men like yourself, men who would not dare insult a girl who had friends to protect her."

"You are ungenerous!" he said hotly.

She seemed to start a little. She looked at him, and her beautiful eyes narrowed. Then, without another word, she turned towards the door.

The scene was over, yet he felt no relief.

"Miss Meredyth!"

She did not hear, or affected not to. She turned the handle of the door, but hesitated for a moment. She looked back at him, contempt in her gaze.

"You are ungenerous," he said again. He had not meant to say it; he had to say something, and it seemed to him that her anger against him was almost unreasonable.

She made no answer; the door closed on her, and he was left to try and collect his thoughts.

And he had not even apologised, he reflected now. She had not given him an opportunity to.

Pacing the room, Hugh decided what he would do. He would give her time to cool down, for her wrath to evaporate, then he would seek her out, and tell her as much as he could—tell her that the secret was not entirely his own. He would appeal to the generosity that he had told her she did not possess.

"Hugh!"

"Eh?" He started.

"What does this mean? You don't mean to tell me, Hugh, that all my efforts have gone for nothing?"

Lady Linden had sailed into the room; she was angry, she quivered with rage.

"I take an immense amount of trouble to bring two foolish young people together again, and—and this is the result!"

"What's the result?"

"She has gone!"

"Oh!"

"Did you know she had gone?"

"No, I knew nothing at all about her."

"Well, she has. She left the house twenty minutes ago. I've sent Chepstow after her in the car; he is to ask her to return."

"I don't suppose she will," Hugh said, remembering the very

Henry St. John Cooper

firm look about Miss Joan Meredyth's mouth.

"And I planned the reconciliation, I made sure that once you came face to face it would be all right. Hugh, there is more behind all this than meets the eye!"

"That's it," he said, "a great deal more! No third person can interfere with any hope of success."

"And you," she said, "can let a girl like that, your own wife, go out of your life and make no effort to detain her!"

He nodded.

"For two pins," said Lady Linden, "I would box your ears, Hugh Alston."

# CHAPTER V

## "PERHAPS I SHALL GO BACK"

Perhaps she was over-sensitive and a little unreasonable, but she would not admit it. She had been insulted by a man who had used her name lightly, who had proclaimed that he was her husband, a man who was a complete stranger to her. She had heard of him before from Marjorie Linden, when they were at school together.

Marjorie had spoken of this man in effusive admiration. Joan's lips curled with scorn. She did not question her own anger. She did not ask herself, was it reasonable? Had not the man some right to defend himself, to explain? If he had wanted to explain, he had had ample opportunity, and he had not taken advantage of it. No, it was a joke—a cruel, cowardly joke at her expense.

Poor and alone in the world, with none to defend her, she had been subjected to the odious attentions of Slotman. She was ready to regard all men as creatures of the same type. She had allowed poverty to narrow her views and warp her mind, and now—

"I beg your pardon, ma'am—"

　　　　　　　Henry St. John Cooper

She was walking along the road to the station. She turned, a man had pulled up in a small car; he touched his hat.

"My lady sent me after you, Mrs. Alston."

Joan gripped her hands tightly. She looked with blazing eyes at the man—"Mrs. Alston..." Even the servant!

"My lady begs that you will return with me. She would be very much hurt, ma'am, if you left the house like this, her ladyship begs me to say."

"Who was your message for?"

"For you, ma'am, of course," said the man.

"Ma'am—Mrs. Alston!" So this joke had been passed on even to the servants, and now she was asked to return.

"Go back and tell Lady Linden that I do not understand her message in the least. Kindly say that the person you overtook on the road was Miss Joan Meredyth, who is taking the next train to London." She bent her head, turned her back on him, and made her way on to the station.

Half an hour later she was leaning back wearily on the dusty seat of a third-class railway carriage, on her way back to the London she hated. Now she was going back again, because she had nowhere else to go. As she sat there with closed eyes, and the tears on her cheeks, she counted up her resources. They were so small, so slender, yet she had been so careful. And now this useless journey had eaten deeply into the little store.

She had no more than enough to keep her for another week, one more week, and then.... She shivered at the thought of the destitution that was before her.

Dinner at the boarding-house was over when she returned, but its unsavoury and peculiar smell still pervaded the place.

"Why, Miss Meredyth, I thought you were away for the week-end, at least," Mrs. Wenham said. "I suppose you won't want any dinner?"

"No," Joan said. "I shall not want anything. I—I—" She paused. "I was obliged to come back, after all. Perhaps you could let me have a cup of tea in my room, Mrs. Wenham?"

"Well, it's rather inconvenient with all the washing-up to do, and as you know I make it a rule that boarders have to be in to their meals, or go without—still—"

"Please don't trouble!" Joan said stiffly.

The woman looked up the stairs after the tall, slight figure.

"Very well, then, I won't!" she muttered. "The airs some people give themselves! Anyone would think she was a lady, instead of a clerk or something."

There was a letter addressed to Joan waiting for her in her room. She opened it, and read it.

"DEAR JOAN,

"I suppose you are in a temper with me, and I don't think you have acted quite fairly. A man can't do more than ask a girl to be his wife. It is not usually considered an insult; however, I say nothing, except just this: You won't find it easy to get other work to do, and if you like to come back here on Monday morning, the same as usual, I think you

Henry St. John Cooper

will be doing the sensible thing.

"Yours,
"PHILIP SLOTMAN."

She had never meant to go back. This morning she had thanked Heaven that she had looked her last on Mr. Philip Slotman, and yet a few hours can effect such changes.

The door was open to her; she could go back, and pick up her life again where she had dropped it before her journey to Cornbridge. After all, Slotman was not the only cad in the world. She would find others, it seemed to her, wherever she went.

At any rate, Slotman had opened the door by which she might re-enter. As he said, work would be very, very hard to get, and it was a bitter thing to have to starve.

"Perhaps," she said to herself wearily as she lay down on her bed, "perhaps I shall go back. It does not seem to matter so very much after all what I do—and I thought it did."

# CHAPTER VI

## "THE ONLY POSSIBLE THING"

For the first time since when, as a small, curly-headed boy, Hugh Alston had looked up at her ladyship with unclouded fearless eyes, that had appealed instantly to her, he and she were bad friends. Hugh had driven back to Hurst Dormer after a brief battle with her ladyship. He had seen Marjorie for a few moments, had soothed her, and told her not to worry, that it was not her fault. He had kissed her in brotherly fashion, and had wondered a little at himself for the slight feeling of impatience against her that came to him. He had never been impatient of her before, but her tears this afternoon unreasonably annoyed him.

"She's a dear, sweet little soul, and over tender-hearted. Of course, she got me into this mess, and of course, bless her heart, she is worrying over it; but it can't be helped. As for that other girl!" His lips tightened. It seemed to him that Miss Joan Meredyth had not shone any more than he had. She had taken the whole thing in bad part.

"No woman," said Hugh to himself, "has any sense of humour!" In which he was wrong, besides which, it had nothing to do with the case.

Henry St. John Cooper

"I am disappointed in Hugh," Lady Linden said to her niece. "I don't often admit myself wrong; in this matter I do. I regarded Hugh Alston as a man utterly and completely open and above board. I find him nothing of the kind. I am deeply disappointed. I am glad to feel that my plans with regard to Hugh Alston and yourself will come to nothing."

"But, aunt—"

"Hold your tongue! and don't interrupt me when I am speaking. I have been considering the matter of you and Tom Arundel. Of course, your income is a small one, even if I released it, but—"

"Aunt—we—we wouldn't mind, I could manage on so little. I should love to manage for him." The girl clasped her hands, she looked with pleading eyes at the old lady.

"Well, well, we shall see!" her ladyship said indulgently. "I don't say No, and I don't say Yes. You are both young yet. By the way, write a letter to Tom and ask him to dine with us to-morrow."

"Thank you, aunt!" Marjorie flushed to her eyes. "Oh, thank you so much!"

"My good girl, there's nothing to get excited about. I don't suppose that he will eat more than about half a crown's worth."

Meanwhile, Hugh Alston had retired to his house at Hurst Dormer in a none too happy frame of mind. He had rowed with Lady Linden, had practically told her to mind her own business, which was a thing everyone had been wishing she would do for the past ten years, and no one had ever dared tell her to.

Altogether, he felt miserably unhappy, furious with himself and angry with Miss Joan Meredyth. The one and only person he did not blame was the one, only and entirely, to blame—Marjorie!

This Sunday morning Hugh in his study heard the chug-chug of a small and badly driven light car, and looked out of the window to see Marjorie stepping out of the vehicle.

"Hugh," she said a few moments later, "I am so—so worried about you. I hate to think that all this trouble is through me. Aunt thinks I have gone to church, but I haven't. I got out the car, and drove here myself. Hugh, what can I do?"

"There's one thing you can't do, child, and that is drive a car! There are heaps of things you can do. One of them is to go back and be happy, and not worry your little head over anything."

"But I must, it is all because of me; and, Hugh, aunt has asked Tom to dinner to-day."

"I hope he has a good dinner," said Hugh.

"Hugh!" She looked at him. "It is no good trying to make light of it. I know you've been worried. I know you and—and Joan must have had a scene yesterday, or she wouldn't have left the house without even seeing me."

"We had—a few words; I noticed that she did seem a little angry," he said.

"Poor Joan! She was always so terribly proud; it was her poverty that made her proud and sensitive, I think."

He nodded. "I think so, too. Poverty inclines her to take an

Henry St. John Cooper

exaggerated view of everything, Marjorie. She took it badly."

The girl slipped her hand through his arm. "Is—is there anything I can do? It is all my fault, Hugh. Shall I confess to aunt, and then go and see Joan, and—"

"Not on your life, you'll spoil everything. I am out of favour with the old lady; she will take Tom into favour in my place. All will go well with you and Tom, and after all that is what I worked for. With regard to Miss Joan Meredyth—" He paused.

"Yes, Hugh, what about Joan? Oh, Hugh, now you have seen her, don't you think she is wonderful?"

"I thought she had a very unpleasing temper," he said.

"There isn't a sweeter girl in the world," Marjorie said.

"I didn't notice any particular sweetness about her yesterday. She had reason, of course, to feel annoyed, but I think she made the most of it, however—" He paused.

"Yes, Hugh, what shall you do? I know you have something in your mind."

"You are right; I have. I am going to do the only thing that seems to me possible just now."

"And that is?"

"Seek out Miss Joan Meredyth, and ask her to become my wife in reality."

# CHAPTER VII

## MR. SLOTMAN ARRIVES AT
## A MISUNDERSTANDING

At half-past nine on the Monday morning Miss Joan Meredyth walked into Mr. Slotman's office, and Mr. Slotman, seeing her, turned his head aside to hide the smirk of satisfaction.

"Women," he said to himself, "are all alike. They give themselves confounded airs and graces, but when it comes to the point, they aren't born fools. She knows jolly well she wouldn't get another job in a hurry, and here she is."

But Mr. Slotman made up his mind to go cautiously and carefully. He would not let Miss Meredyth witness his sense of satisfaction.

"I am glad you have returned, Miss Meredyth. I felt sure that you would; there's no reason whatever we shouldn't get on perfectly well."

The girl gave him a stiff little inclination of her head. She had done much personal violence to her sense of pride, yet she had come back because the alternative—worklessness, possible starvation and homelessness—had not appealed to her. And, after all, knowing Mr. Slotman to be what he was, she was forewarned and forearmed.

So Joan came back and took up her old work, and Mr. Slotman practised temporarily a courtesy and a forbearance that were foreign to him. But Mr. Slotman had by no means given up his hopes and desires. Joan appealed to him as no woman ever had. He admired her statuesque beauty. He admired her air of breeding; he admired the very pride that she had attempted to crush him with.

A woman like that could go anywhere, Slotman thought, and pictured it to himself, he following in her trail, and finding an entry into a society that would have otherwise resolutely shut him out. For like most men of his type, self made, egregious, and generally offensive, he had an inborn desire to get into Society and mingle with his betters.

On the Monday morning there had been delivered to Hugh Alston by hand a little note from Marjorie; it was on pink paper, and was scented delicately. If he had not been so very much in love with Marjorie, the pink notepaper might have annoyed him, but it did not. The faint fragrance reminded him of her.

She wrote a neat and exquisite hand; everything that she did was neat and exquisite, and remembering his hopes of not so long ago, he groaned a little dismally to himself as he reverently cut the envelope.

"MY DEAR HUGH,

"I have managed to get the address from aunt. It is 'Miss Joan Meredyth, care Mrs. Wenham, No. 7, Bemrose Square, London, W.C.' I have been thinking so much about what you said, and hoping that your plan may succeed. I am sure that you would be very, very happy together...."

(Hugh laughed unmusically.)

"Tom has been here all the afternoon and evening, and aunt has been perfectly charming to him. Hugh, I know that everything is going to be right now, and I owe it all to you. You don't know how grateful I am, dear. I shall never, never forget your goodness and sweetness to me, dear old Hugh.

"Your loving
"MARJORIE."

With something approaching reverent care, Hugh put the little pink-scented note into his pocket-book.

To-night he would go to Town, to-morrow he would interview Miss Joan Meredyth. He would offer her no explanations, because the secret was not his own, and nothing must happen now that might upset or tell against Marjorie's happiness.

He would express regret for what had happened, ask her to try and realise that no indignity and no insult had ever been intended against her, and then he would offer her his hand, but certainly not his heart. If she felt the sting of her poverty so, then perhaps the thought of his eight thousand a year would act as balm to her wounded feelings.

At this time Hugh Alston had a very poor opinion of Miss Meredyth. He did not deny her loveliness. He could not; no man in his senses and gifted with eyesight could. But the placid prettiness of Marjorie appealed to him far more than the cold, disdainful beauty of the young woman he had called ungenerous, and who had in her turn called him a cad.

It was Mrs. Wenham herself who opened the hall door of the house in Bemrose Square to Mr. Hugh Alston at noon on the day following.

Though certainly not dressed in the height of fashion, and by no means an exquisite, Mr. Hugh Alston had that about him that suggested birth and large possessions. Mrs. Wenham beamed on him, cheating herself for a moment into the belief that he had come to add one more to the select circle of persons she alluded to as her "paying guests."

Her face fell a little when he asked for Miss Meredyth.

"Oh, Miss Meredyth has gone to work," she said.

"To work?"

"Yes, she's a clerk or something in the City. The office is that of Philip Slotman and Company, Number sixteen, Gracebury."

"You think that I could see her there?" asked Hugh, who had little knowledge of City offices and their routine and rules, so far as hirelings are concerned.

"I suppose you could; you are a friend of hers?"

He nodded.

"Well, I don't know that it is usual for visitors to call on lady clerks. If I might make a suggestion I'd say send in your card to Mr. Slotman, and ask his permission to see Miss Meredyth."

"Thanks!" Hugh said. "If that's the right thing to do, I'll do it."

Half an hour later Mr. Slotman was examining Hugh's card.

"Who is he?"

"A tall, well-dressed gentleman, sir; young. Looks as if he's up from the country, but he's a gentleman all right," the clerk said.

"Very good, I'll see him."

Slotman rose as Hugh came in. He recognised the man of position and possessions, a man of the class that Slotman always cultivated.

"I wish to ask your permission to interview Miss Meredyth. I understand that, in business hours, the permission of the employer should be asked first."

"Delighted!" Slotman said. "You are a friend of Miss Meredyth's?" He looked keenly at Hugh, and the first spark of jealousy was ignited in his system.

"Hardly that, an acquaintance only," said Hugh.

Slotman felt relieved.

"Miss Meredyth is in the outer general office. You could hardly talk to her there. If you will sit down, I will go out and send her to you, Mr.—Alston." He glanced at the card.

"Thanks, perhaps you would be so kind as not to mention my name to her," said Hugh.

"Something up!" Slotman thought. He was an eminently suspicious man; he suspected everyone, and more particularly all those who were in his pay. He suspected his clerks of wasting their time—his time, the time he paid for. He suspected them of filching the petty cash, stealing the postage stamps, cheating him and getting the better of him in some way, and in order to keep a watch on them he had riddled his suite of offices with peepholes, listening holes, and spyholes in every unlikely corner.

A small waiting office divided his private apartment from the General Office, and peepholes cunningly contrived permitted anyone to hear and see all that passed in the General Office, and in his own office too.

He found a young clerk in the waiting office, and sent him to Miss Meredyth.

"Ask Miss Meredyth to go to my office at once, not through this way, and then you remain in the General Office till I send for you," said Slotman.

This gave him the advantage he wanted. He locked both doors leading into the waiting office, and took up his position at the spyhole that gave him command of his own office.

He could see his visitor plainly. Hugh Alston was pacing the room slowly, his hands behind his back, his face wearing a look of worry. Slotman saw him pause and turn expectantly to the door at the far end of the room.

Slotman could not see this door, but he heard it open, and he knew by the look on the man's face that Joan had come in.

"Why are you here? How dare you follow me here?"

"I have dared to follow you here, to express my deep regret for what is past," Hugh said. He looked at the girl, her white face, the hard line made by a mouth that should be sweet and gentle.

It seemed, he thought, that the very sight of him roused all that was cold and bitter in her nature.

"Am I to be tormented and insulted by you all my life?" she asked.

"You are unreasonable! You cannot think that this visit is one that gives me any pleasure," Hugh said.

"Then why do you come?"

"I asked permission of your employer to see you, and he kindly placed his office at our disposal. I shall not keep you long."

"I do not intend that you shall, and in future—"

"Will you hear what I have to say? Surely I am not asking too much?"

"Is it necessary?"

"To me, very! I wish to make a few things plain to you. In the past—I had no intention of hurting or of disgracing you—"

Slotman started, and clenched his hands. What did that man mean? He wondered, what could such words as those mean?

"But as I have shamed and angered you, I have come to offer the only reparation in my power—a poor one, I will admit."

He looked at her, paused for a moment to give her an

opportunity of speaking, but she did not speak. She looked at him steadily.

"May I briefly explain my position? I am practically alone in the world. My home is at Hurst Dormer, one of the finest old buildings in Sussex. I have an income of eight thousand a year."

"What has this to do with me?"

"Only that I am offering it to you, myself and all I possess. I am asking you to do me the honour of marrying me. It seems to me that it is the one and the only atonement that I can make for what has passed."

"You are—very generous! And—and you think that I would accept?"

"I hoped that you might consider the offer."

Slotman gripped at the edge of the table against which he leaned.

He could scarcely believe his own ears—Joan, who had held her head so high, whom he had believed to be above the breath of suspicion!

If it were possible for such a man as Mr. Philip Slotman to be shocked, then Slotman was deeply shocked at this moment. He had come to regard Joan as something infinitely superior to himself. Self-indulgent, a libertine, he had pursued her with his attentions, pestered her with his admiration and his offensive compliments. Then it had slowly dawned on the brain of Mr. Philip Slotman that this girl was something better, higher, purer than most women he had known. He had come to realise it little by little. His feelings towards her had undergone a change. The idea of marriage had come to him, a thing he had never considered seriously before. Little by little it grew on him that he would prefer to have Joan Meredyth for a wife rather than in any other capacity. He could have been so proud of her beauty, her birth and her breeding.

And now everything had undergone a change. The bottom had fallen out of his little world of romance. He stood there, gasping and clutching at the edge of the table, while he listened to the man in the adjoining room offering marriage to Joan Meredyth "as the only possible atonement" he could make her!

Naturally, Mr. Philip Slotman could not understand in the least why or wherefore; it was beyond his comprehension.

And now he stood listening eagerly, holding his breath waiting for her answer.

Would she take him, this evidently rich man? If so, then good-bye to all his hopes, all his chances.

Within the room the two faced one another in momentary silence. A flush had come into the girl's cheeks, making her adorable. For an instant the coldness and hardness and bitterness were all gone, and Hugh Alston had a momentary glimpse of the real woman, the woman who was neither hard, nor cold, but was womanly and sweet and tender.

And then she was her old self again, the bitterness and the anger had come back.

"I thank you for making everything so clear to me, your wealth and position and your desire to make—to make amends for the insult and the shame you have put on me. I need hardly say of course that I refuse!"

"Why?"

"Did you ever expect me to accept? I think you did not!"

She gave him a slight inclination of the head and, turning, went out of the room, and Hugh Alston stood staring at the door that had closed on her.

# CHAPTER VIII

## THE DREAM GIRL

"She is utterly without generosity; she is cold and hard and bitter, and she has made a mountain out of a molehill, built up a great grievance on what was, after all, only a foolish and ill-considered statement. She is pleased to feel herself deeply insulted, and she hates me for what I did in perfect innocence. I have done all that I can do. I have offered to make amends in the only way I can think of, and she refuses to accept either that or my apologies. Very well, then... But what a lovely face it is, and for just that moment, when the hardness and bitterness were gone..." He paused; his own face softened. One could not be angry for long with a vision like that, which was passing before his mind, conjured up by memory.

Just for that instant, when the flush had come into her cheeks, she had looked all those things that she was not—sweet, womanly, tender, and gentle, a woman with an immense capacity for love.

"Bah!" said Hugh. "I'm an idiot. I shall go to a theatre to-night, forget all about her, and go home to-morrow—home." He sighed a little drearily. For months past he had pictured pretty Marjorie Linden as queen of that home, and now he

Henry St. John Cooper

knew that it would never be. His house would remain lonely and empty, as must his life be.

He sighed sentimentally, and took out Marjorie's little pink note from his pocket-book. He noticed for the first time that it was somewhat over-scented. He realised that he did not like the smell of scent, especially on notepaper, and pink was not his favourite colour. In fact, he disliked pink. Marjorie was happy, Lady Linden was beaming on Tom Arundel, the cloud had lifted from Marjorie's life. Hugh tore up the pink, smelly little missive, and dropped the fragments into the grate of the hotel bedroom.

"That's that!" he said. "And it's ended and done with!"

He was amazed to find himself not broken-hearted and utterly cast down. He lighted his pipe and puffed hard, to destroy the lingering smell of the pink notepaper. Then he laughed gently.

"By every right I should now be on my way to the bar to drown dull care in drink. She's a dear little soul, the sweetest and dearest and best in the world. I hope Tom Arundel will appreciate her and make the little thing happy. I would have done my best, but somehow I feel that Tom is the better man, so far as Marjorie is concerned."

Grey eyes, not disdainful and cold and scornful, but soft, and filled with kindliness and gentleness, banished all memory of Marjorie's pretty pathetic blue eyes. Why, Hugh thought, had that girl looked at him like that for just one moment? Why had she appeared for that instant so different? It was as if a cold and bitter mask had fallen from her face, and he had had a peep at the true—the real woman, the woman all love and tenderness and gentleness, behind it.

"Anyhow, it doesn't matter," said Hugh. "I've done what I believed to be the right thing. She turned me down; the affair is now closed, and we'll think of something else."

But it was not easy. At his dinner, which he took in solitary state, he had a companion, a girl with grey eyes and flushed cheeks who sat opposite to him at the table. She said nothing, but she looked at him, and the beauty of her intoxicated him, and the smile of her found an answer on his own lips. She ate nothing, nor did the waiter see her; so far as the waiter was concerned, there was an empty chair, but Hugh Alston saw her.

"Why," he asked, "why can you look like that, and yet be so different? That look in your eyes makes you the most beautiful and wonderful thing in this world, and yet..."

He laughed softly to himself. He was uttering his thoughts aloud, and the unromantic waiter stared at him.

"Beg your pardon, sir?" he asked.

"That's all right!" Hugh said. "What won the three-thirty?"

"I don't think there was any racing to-day, sir," the man said.

He went away, not completely satisfied as to this visitor's sanity, and Hugh drifted back into dreams and memories.

"You are very wonderful," he said to himself, "yet you made me very angry; you hurt me and made me furious. I called you ungenerous, and I meant it, and so you were. Yet when you look at me with your eyes like that and the colour in your cheeks, I can't find one word to say against you."

He went to the theatre that night. It was a successful play. All London was talking of it, but Hugh Alston never remembered what it was about. He was thinking of a girl with cold disdainful looks that changed suddenly to softness and tenderness. She sat beside him as she had sat opposite to him at dinner. On the stage the actors talked meaningless stuff; nothing was real, save this girl beside him.

"What's the matter with you, my good fellow, is," Hugh said to himself, as he walked back to the hotel that night, "you're a fickle man; you don't know your own mind. A week ago you were dreaming of Marjorie; you considered blue eyes the most beautiful thing in the world. You would not have listened to the claims of eyes of any other colour, and now— Bless her dear little heart, she'll be happy as the day is long with Tom Arundel, with his nice fair hair parted down the middle, and her pretty scented notepaper. Of course she'll be happy. She would have been miserable at Hurst Dormer, and so should I have been; seeing her miserable, I should have been miserable myself. But I shall go back to Hurst Dormer to-morrow and start on that renovation work. It will give me something to occupy my time and attention."

That night, much to his surprise, Hugh found he could not sleep.

"It's the strange bed," he said. "It's the noise of the London streets." Sleeplessness had never troubled him before, but to-night he rolled and tossed from side to side, and then at last he sat bolt upright in the bed.

"Good Lord!" he said. "Good Lord, it can't be!" He stared into the thick darkness and saw an oval face, crowned by waving brown hair, that glinted gold in the highlights. He saw a sweet, womanly, tender, smiling mouth and a pair of grey eyes that seemed to burn into his own.

"It can't be!" he said again. And yet it was!

# CHAPTER IX

## THE PEACEMAKER

"Bless my soul!" said General Bartholomew. He had turned to the last page and looked at the signature. "Alicia Linden! I haven't heard a word of her for five and twenty years. A confoundedly handsome girl she was too. Hudson, where's my glasses?"

"Here, General," said the young secretary.

The General put them on.

"My dear George," he read.

It was a long letter, four pages closely written in Lady Linden's strong, almost masculine hand.

"...I remember that when she visited me years ago, she told that me you were an old friend of her father's. This being so, I think you should combine with me in trying to bring these two wrong-headed young people together. I have quarrelled with Hugh Alston, so I can do nothing at the moment; but you, being on the spot so to speak, in London, and Hugh I understand also being in London..."

Henry St. John Cooper

"What the dickens is the woman drivelling about?" the General demanded. "Hudson!"

"Yes, sir!"

"Read this letter carefully, digest it, and then briefly explain to me what the dickens it is all about."

The secretary took the letter and read it carefully.

"This letter is from Lady Linden, of Cornbridge Manor House, Cornbridge. She is deeply interested in a young lady, Miss Joan Meredyth. At least—" Hudson paused.

"Joan, pretty little Joan Meredyth—old Tom Meredyth's girl. Yes, go on!"

"Three years ago," Hudson went on, "Miss Meredyth was married in secret to a Mr. Hugh Alston—"

"Hugh Alston, of course—bless me, I know of Hugh Alston! Isn't he the son of old George Alston, of Hurst Dormer?"

"Yes, that would be the man, sir. Her ladyship speaks of Mr. Alston's house, Hurst Dormer."

"That's the man then, that's the man!" said the General, delighted by his own shrewdness. "So little Joan married him. Well, what about it?"

"They parted, sir, almost at once, having quarrelled bitterly. Lady Linden does not say what about, and they have never been together since. A little while ago she received a letter from Miss Meredyth, as she still continues to call herself, asking her assistance in finding work for her to do. And that reminds me, General, that a similar letter was addressed to you by Miss Meredyth, which I sent on to you at Harrogate."

"Must have got there after I left. I never had it—go on!"

"Lady Linden urges you to do something for the young lady, and do all in your power to bring her and Mr. Alston together. She says if you could effect a surprise meeting between them, good may come of it. She is under the impression that they will not meet intentionally. Miss Meredyth's address is, 7 Bemrose Square, and Mr. Alston is staying at The Northborough Hotel, St. James. Of course, there is a good deal besides in the letter, General—"

"Of course!" the General said. "There always is. Well, Hudson, we must do something. I knew the girl's father, and the boy's too. Tom Meredyth was a fine fellow, reckless and a spendthrift, by George! but as straight a man and as true a gentleman as ever walked. And old George Alston was one of my best friends, Hudson. We must do something for these two young idiots."

"Very good, sir!" said Hudson. "How shall we proceed?"

The General did not answer; he sat deep in thought.

"Hudson, I am getting to be a forgetful old fool," he said. "I'm getting old, that's what it is. Before I went to Harrogate I was with Rankin, my solicitor. He was talking to me about the Meredyths. I forget exactly what it was, but there's some money coming to the girl from Bob Meredyth, who went out to Australia. No, I forget, but some money I know, and now the girl apparently wants it, if she is asking for influence to get work. Go and ring Rankin up on the telephone. Don't tell him we know where Joan Meredyth is, but give him my compliments, and ask him to repeat what he told me the other day."

Hudson went out. He was gone ten minutes, while the General dozed in a chair. He was thinking of the past, of those good old days when he and Tom Meredyth, the girl's father, and George Alston, the lad's father, were all young fellows together. Ah, good old days, fine old days! When the young blood coursed strong and hot in the veins, when there was no need of Harrogate waters, when the limbs were supple and strong, and the eyes bright and clear. "And they are gone," the old man muttered—"both of them, and a lot of other good fellows besides; and I am an old, old man, begad, an old fellow sitting here waiting for my call to come and—" He paused, and looked up.

"Well, Hudson?"

"I have been speaking to Mr. Rankin, sir. He wished me to tell you—" Hudson paused; his face was a little flushed, as with some inward excitement.

"Go on!"

"Before his death, which occurred six months ago, Mr. Robert Meredyth, who had made a great deal of money in Australia, re-purchased the old Meredyth family estate at Starden in Kent, Starden Hall, meaning to return to England, and take up his residence there. Unfortunately, he died on board ship. His wife was dead, his only son was killed in the war, and he had left the whole of his fortune, about three hundred thousand pounds, and the Starden Hall Estate, to his niece, Miss Joan Meredyth."

"By George! so the girl's an heiress!"

"And a very considerable one!"

"We won't say a word about it—not a word, Hudson. We'll

get the girl here, and patch up this quarrel between her and her young husband. When that's done we'll spring the news on 'em, eh?"

"I think it would be a good idea, General," Hudson said.

# CHAPTER X

## "IN SPITE OF EVERYTHING"

Slotman leaned across his table. His eyes were glaring his face was flushed a dusky red.

Against the wall, her face white as death, but her eyes unafraid, the girl stood staring at him, in silent amazement.

"And you—you've given yourself airs, set yourself up to be all that you are not! You've held me at arm's length, and all the time—all the time you're nothing—nothing!" the man shouted. "I know all about you! I know that a man offered you marriage to atone for the past—to atone—you hear me? I tell you I know about you, and yet you dare—dare to give yourself airs—dare to pretend to be a monument of innocence—you!"

"You are mad!" the girl said quietly.

"Yes, that's it—mad—mad for you! Mad with love for you!" Slotman laughed sharply. "I'm a fool—a blind, mad fool; but you've got me as no other woman ever did. I tell you I know about you and the past, but it shall make no difference. I repeat my offer now—I'll marry you, in spite of everything!"

It seemed to Joan that a kind of madness came to her, born of her fear and her horror of this man.

She forced her way past him, and gained the door, how she scarcely remembered. She could only recall a great and burning sense of rage and shame. She remembered seeing, as in some distant vision, a man with scared eyes and sagging jaw—a man who, an utter coward by nature, had given way at her approach, whose passion had melted into fear—fear followed later by senseless rage against himself and against her.

So she had made her retreat from the office of Mr. Philip Slotman, and had shaken the dust of the place off her feet.

It was all very well to bear up and show a brave and determined face to the enemy, to give no sign of weakness when the danger threatened. But now, alone in her own room in the lodging-house, she broke down, as any sensitive, highly strung woman might.

Joan looked at her face in the glass. She looked at it critically. Was it the face, she asked herself, of a girl who invited insult? For insult on insult had been heaped on her. She had been made the butt of one man's senseless joke or lie, whatever it might be; the butt of another man's infamous passion.

"Oh!" she said, "Oh!" She clasped her cheeks between her hands, and stared at her reflection with wide grey eyes. "I hate myself! I hate this face of mine that invites such—such—" She shuddered, and moaned softly to herself.

Beauty, why should women want it, unless they are rich and well placed, carefully protected? Beauty to a poor girl is added danger. She would be a thousand, a million times better and happier without it.

She grew calmer presently. She must think. To-morrow the money for her board here would be due, and she had not enough to pay. She would not ask Slotman for the wages for this week, never would she ask anything of that man, never see him again.

Then what lay before her? She sat down and put her elbows on the dressing table with its dingy cheap lace cover, and in doing so her eyes fell on a letter, a letter that had been placed here for her.

It was from General Bartholomew, an answer to the appeal she had written him at the same time that she had written to Lady Linden. It came now, kindly, friendly and even affectionate, at the very eleventh hour.

"I was away, my dear child, when your letter came. It was forwarded to Harrogate to me. Now I am back in London again. Your father was my very dear friend; his daughter has a strong claim on me, so pack your things, my dear, and come to me at once. I am an old fellow, old enough to have been your father's father, and the little note that I enclose must be accepted, as it is offered, in the same spirit of affection. It will perhaps settle your immediate necessities. To-morrow morning I shall send for you, so have all your things ready, and believe me.

"Yours affectionately,
"GEORGE BARTHOLOMEW."

She cried over the letter, the proud head drooped over it; bright tears streamed from the grey eyes.

Could Hugh Alston have seen her now, her face softened by

the gladness and the gratitude that had come to her, he would have seen in her the woman of his dreams.

The banknote would clear everything. She did not scruple to accept it in the spirit of affection in which it was offered. It would have been churlish and false pride to refuse.

He had said that he would send for her when the morning came; he had taken it for granted that she would go, and there was no need to answer the letter. And when the morning came she was ready and waiting, her things packed, her last bill to Mrs. Wenham paid.

The maid came tapping on the door.

"Someone waiting for you, miss, in the drawing-room."

Joan went down. It would be the old fellow, the warm-hearted old man himself come to fetch her! She entered the big ugly room, with its dingy wall-paper and threadbare carpet, its oleographs in tarnished frames, its ancient centre ottoman, its elderly piano and unsafe, uncertain chairs. How she hated this room, where of evenings the 'paying guests' distorted themselves.

But she came into it now eagerly, with bright eyes and flushed cheeks, and hand held out, only to draw back with sudden chill.

It was Mr. Philip Slotman who rose from the ottoman.

"Joan, I've come to tell you I am sorry, sorry and ashamed," he said. "I was mad. I want you to forgive me."

"There need be no talk of forgiveness," she said. "You are the type of man one can perhaps forget—never forgive!"

He winced a little, and his face changed to a dusky red.

"I said more than I meant to say. But what I said, after all, was right enough. I know more about you than I think you guess. I know about that fellow, that—what's his name?—Alston—who came. I know why he came."

"You are a friend of his, perhaps? I am not surprised."

"I never saw him before in my life, but I know all about him—and you—all the same. He was willing to act fairly to you after all, and—"

"What is this to do with you?" she asked.

"A lot!" he said thickly. "A lot! Look here!" He took another step towards her. "Last night I behaved like a mad fool. I—I said more than I meant to say. I—I saw you, and I thought of that fellow—and—and you, and it drove me mad!"

"Why?" She was looking at him with calm eyes of contempt, the same look that she had given to Hugh Alston at their last meeting.

"Why—why?" he said. "Why?" He clenched his hands. "You know why, you know I love you! I want you! I'll marry you! I'll dig a hole and bury the past in it—curse the past! I'll say nothing more, Joan. I swear before Heaven I'll never try and dig up the past again. I forgive everything!"

"You—you forgive everything?" Her eyes blazed. "What have you to forgive? What right have you to tell me that you forgive—me?"

"I can't let you go, I can't! Joan, I tell you I'll never throw the past in your face. I'll forget Alston and—"

The door behind the girl opened, the maid appeared.

"Miss," she said, "there's a car waiting down below. The man says he is from General Bartholomew, and he has come for you."

"Thank you. I am coming now. My luggage is ready, Annie. Can you get someone to carry it down?"

Joan moved to the door. She looked back at Slotman. "I hope," she said quietly, "that we shall never meet again, Mr. Slotman, and I wish you good morning!" And then she was gone.

Slotman walked to the window. He looked down and saw a car, by no means a cheap car, and he knew the value of things, none better. He waited, unauthorised visitor as he now was, and saw the girl come out, saw the liveried chauffeur touch his cap to her and hold the door for her, saw her enter. Presently he saw luggage brought down and placed on the roof of the limousine, and then the car drove away.

Slotman rubbed his chin thoughtfully. "Well, I'll be hanged! And who the dickens is General Bartholomew? And why should she go to him, luggage and all? Is it anything to do with that fellow Alston? Has she accepted his offer after all?" He shook his head. "No, I don't think so."

The General put his two hands on Joan's shoulders. He looked at her, and then he kissed her.

"You are very welcome, my dear," he said. "I blame myself, I do indeed. I ought to have found out where you were long ago. Your father was one of my dearest friends, God rest his soul. I knew him well, and his dear little wife too—your mother, my child, one of the loveliest women I ever saw.

And you are like her, as like her as a daughter can be like her mother. Bless my heart, it takes me back when I see you, takes me back to the day when Tom married her, the loveliest girl—but I am forgetting, I am forgetting. You've brought your things?" he asked. "Hudson, where's Hudson? Ring for Mrs. Weston, that's my housekeeper, child. She'll look after you. And now you are here, you will stay here with us for a long time, a very long time. It can't be too long, my dear. I am a lonely old man, but we'll do our best to make you happy."

"I think," Joan said softly, "that you have done that already! Your welcome and your kindness, have made me happier than I have been for a very, very long time."

# CHAPTER XI

## THE GENERAL CALLS ON HUGH

Hugh Alston lingered in London, why, he would not admit, even to himself. In reality he had lingered on in the hope of seeing Joan Meredyth again. How he should see her, where and when, he had not the faintest idea; but he wanted to see her even more than he wanted to see Hurst Dormer.

He had thought of going to the city and calling on Mr. Philip Slotman again. But he had not liked Mr. Slotman.

"If I see her, she will only suggest that I am annoying and insulting her," Hugh thought. "I suppose I thought that I was doing a very fine and very clever thing in asking her to be my wife!" His face burned at the thought. He had meant it well; but, looking back, it struck him that he had acted like a conceited fool. He had thought to make all right, by bestowing all his possessions and his person on her, and she had put him in his place, had declined even without thanks.

"And serve me jolly well right!" Hugh said. "Who?" he added aloud.

"Gentleman, sir—General Bartholomew," said the hotel page.

Henry St. John Cooper

"And who on earth is he?"

"Short, stout gentleman, sir, white whiskers."

"That's quite satisfactory then; I'll see him," said Hugh.

He found the General in the lounge.

"You're Hugh Alston," said the General. "I'd know you anywhere. You are your father over again. I hope that you are as good a man."

"I wish I could think so," Hugh said, "but I can't!" He shook hands with the General. He had a dim recollection of the old fellow, as one of his father's friends, who in the old days, when he was a child, had come down to Hurst Dormer; but the recollection was dim.

"How did you find me out here, sir?"

"Ah, ha! That's it—just a piece of luck! The name struck me—Alston—I thought of George Alston. I said to myself, 'Can this be his boy?' And you are, eh? George Alston, of Hurst Dormer."

The General rambled on, but he forgot to explain to Hugh how it was that he had found him out at the Northborough Hotel, and presently Hugh forgot to enquire, which was what the General wanted.

"You'll dine with me to-night, eh? I won't take no— understand. I want to talk over old times!"

"I thought of returning to Sussex to-night," said Hugh.

"Not to be thought of! I can't let you go! I shall expect you at seven."

The old fellow seemed to be so genuinely anxious, so kindly, so friendly, that Hugh had not the heart to refuse him.

"Very well, sir; it is good of you. I'll come, I'll put off going till to-morrow. I remember you well now, you used to come for the shooting when I was a nipper."

Not till after the old fellow had gone did Hugh wonder how he had unearthed him here in the Northborough Hotel. He had meant to ask him—he had asked him actually, and the General had not explained. But it did not matter, after all. Some coincidence, some easily understandable explanation, of course, would account for it.

"And to-morrow I shall go back," Hugh thought, as he drove to the General's house in a taxicab. "I shall go back to Hurst Dormer, I shall get busy doing something and forget everything that I don't want to remember."

But his thoughts were with the girl he had seen last in Mr. Slotman's office. And he saw her in memory as he had seen her for one brief instant of time—softened and sweetened by some thought, some influence that had come to her for a moment. What influence, what thought, he could not tell; yet, as she had been then, so he saw her always and remembered her.

A respectful manservant took Hugh's coat and hat; he led the way, and flung a door wide.

"General Bartholomew will be with you in a few moments, sir," he said; and Hugh found himself in a large, old-fashioned London drawing-room.

"To-morrow," Hugh was thinking, "Hurst Dormer—work, something to occupy my thoughts till I can forget. It is going to take a lot of forgetting, I suppose I shall feel more or less a cad all my life, though Heaven knows—"

He swung round suddenly. The door had opened; he heard the swish of skirts, and knew it could not be General Bartholomew.

But who it would be he could not have guessed to save his life. They met again for the third time in their lives. At sight of him the girl had started and flushed, had instinctively drawn back. Now she stood still, regarding him with a steadfast stare, the colour slowly fading from her cheeks.

And Hugh stood silent, dumbfounded, astonishment clearly shown on his face.

# CHAPTER XII

## "I TAKE NOT ONE WORD BACK"

"I will do you the justice, Mr. Alston, to believe that you did not anticipate this meeting?"

"You will only be doing me justice if you do not believe it," Hugh said.

The girl bent her proud head. "I did not know that you were a friend of General Bartholomew's?"

"Nor I till to-day, Miss Meredyth."

"I don't understand."

Hugh explained that he had not seen the General since he was a child, till the General had unearthed him at the Northborough Hotel that afternoon.

Joan frowned. Why had the General done that? Why had he, not three minutes ago, patted her on the shoulder, smiled on her, and told her to run down and wait for him in the drawing-room? Suddenly her face burned with a glowing colour. It seemed as if all the world were in league together against her. But this time this man was surely innocent. She had seen the look of astonishment on his face, and knew it for no acting.

"I came here yesterday," she said quietly, "in response to a warm invitation from the General, who was my father's friend."

"My father's too!"

"I—I wanted a home, a friend, and I accepted his invitation eagerly, but since you have come—"

"My presence makes this house impossible for you, of course," Hugh said, and his voice was bitter. "Listen to me, I may never have an opportunity of speaking to you again, Joan." He used her Christian name, scarcely realising that he did so.

"You feel bitterly towards me, and with reason. You have made up your mind that I have deliberately annoyed and insulted you. If you ask me to explain what I did and why I did it, I cannot do so. I have a reason. One day, if I am permitted, I shall be glad to tell you everything. I came here to London like a fool, a senseless, egotistical fool, thinking I should be doing a fine thing, and could put everything right by asking you to become my wife in reality. I can see now what sort of a figure I made of myself, and how I must have appeared to you when I was bragging of my possessions. I suppose I lack a sense of humour, Joan, or there's something wrong with me somewhere. Believe me, senseless and crude as it all was, my intentions were good. I only succeeded in sinking a little lower, if possible, in your estimation, and now I wish to ask your pardon for it."

"I am glad," she said quietly, "that you understand now—"

"I do, and I have felt shame for it. I shall feel better now that I have asked you to forgive. Joan," he went on passionately, "listen! A fool is always hard to separate from his folly. But listen! That day when I saw you in the City, when I made my egregious proposal to you—just for a moment you were touched, something appealed to you. I do not know what it was—my folly, my immense conceit—for which perhaps you pitied me. But it was something, for that one moment I saw you change. The hard look went from your face, a colour came into your cheeks, your eyes grew soft and tender—just for one moment—"

"What does all this—"

"Listen, listen! Let me speak! It may be my last chance. I tell you I saw you as I know you must be—the real woman, not the hard, the condemning judge that you have been to me. And as I saw you for that one moment, I have remembered you and pictured you in my thoughts; and seeing you in memory I have grown to love that woman I saw, to love her with all my heart and soul."

Love! It dawned on her, this man, who had made a sport of her name, was offering her love now! Love! she sickened at the very thought of it—the word had been profaned by Philip Slotman's lips.

"I believe," she thought, "I believe that there is no such thing as love—as holy love, as true, good, sweet love! It is all selfish passion and ugliness!"

"Just now, Mr. Alston"—her voice was cold and scornful, and it chilled him, as one is chilled by a drenching with cold water—"just now you said perhaps you lacked humour. I do not think it is that, I think you have a sense of humour somewhat perverted. Of course, you are only carrying this—

Henry St. John Cooper

this joke one step further—"

"Joan!"

"And as you drove me from Cornbridge Manor, I suppose you will now drive me from this house. Am I to find peace and refuge nowhere, nowhere?"

"If—if you could be generous!" he cried.

She flushed with anger. "You have called me ungenerous before! Am I always to be called ungenerous by you?"

"Forgive me!" His eyes were filled with pleading. He did not know himself, did not recognise the old, happy-go-lucky Hugh Alston, who had accepted many a hard knock from Fate with a smile and a jest.

"And so I am to be driven from this home, this refuge—by you?" she said bitterly. "Oh, have you no sense of manhood in you?"

"I think I have. You shall not be driven away. I, of course, am the one to go. Through me you left Cornbridge, you shall not have to leave this house. I promise you, swear to you, that I shall not darken these doors again. Is that enough? Does that content you?"

"Then I shall have at least something at last to thank you for," she said coldly. And yet, though she spoke coldly, she looked at him and saw something in his face that made her lip tremble. Yet in no other way did she betray her feelings, and he, like the man he was, was of course blind.

It was strange how long they had been left alone, uninterrupted. The strangeness of it did not occur to him, yet it did to her. She turned to the door.

"Joan, wait," he pleaded—"wait! One last word! One day I shall hope to explain to you, then perhaps you will find it in your heart to forgive. For the blunder that I made in Slotman's office, for the further insult, if you look on it as such, I ask you to forgive me now. It was the act of a senseless fool, a mad fool, who had done wrong and tried to do right, and through his folly made matters worse. To-night perhaps I have sinned more than ever before in telling you that I love you. But if that is a sin and past all forgiveness, I glory in it. I take not one word of it back. I shall trouble you no more, and so"—he paused—"so I say good-bye."

"Good-bye!" He held out his hand to her, but she looked him full in the face.

"Good-bye!" she said, and then turned quickly, and in a moment the door was closed between them.

He did not see her hurry away, her hands pressed against her breast. He did not see the face, all womanly and sweet, and soft and tender now. He had only the memory of her brief farewell, the memory of her cold, steady eyes—nothing else beside.

Henry St. John Cooper

# CHAPTER XIII

## THE GENERAL CONFESSES

"My dear, my dear, life is short. I am an old man, and yet looking back it seems but yesterday since I was a boy beginning life. Climbing the hill, my dear, climbing the hill; and when the top was gained, when I stood there in my young manhood, I thought that the world belonged to me. And then the descent, so easy and so swift. The years seem long when one is climbing, but they are as weeks when the top is passed and the descent into the valley begins." He paused. He passed his hand across his forehead. "I meant to speak of something else, of you, child, of your life, of love and happiness, and of those things that should be dear to all us humans."

"I know nothing of love, and of happiness but very, very little," she said.

He took her hand and held it. "You shall know of both!" he promised. "There is strife, there is ill-feeling between you and that lad, your husband."

She wrenched her hand free, her face flushed gloriously.

"You!" she cried. "You too !"

"Yes, I too! I sought him out yesterday, and asked him to this house on purpose that you and he should meet, praying that the meeting might bring peace to you both. I knew the lad's father as I knew yours. Alicia Linden wrote to me and told me all about this unhappy marriage of yours. She told me that she loved you both, that you were both good, that life might be made very happy for you two, but for this misunderstanding—"

"Don't!—don't. Oh, General Bartholomew, how can I make you understand? It is untrue—I am not his wife! I have never been his wife. It was a lie! some foolish joke of his that he will not or cannot explain!"

He looked at her, blinking like one who suddenly finds himself in strong light after the twilight or darkness.

"Not—not married?"

"I never saw that man in my life before I met him at Lady Linden's house, not two weeks ago. All that he has said about our marriage, his and mine, are foolish lies, something beyond my understanding!"

The General waved his hands helplessly.

"It is all extraordinary! Where can that foolish old woman have got hold of this story? What's come to her? She used to be a very clear-minded—"

"It is not she, it is the man—the liar!" Joan cried bitterly. "I tell you I don't understand the reason for it. I cannot understand, I don't believe there is any reason. I believe that it is his idea of humour—I can't even think that he wanted to annoy and shame and anger me as he has, because we were utter strangers."

She stood at the window, looking out into the dull, respectable square. She saw a man ascend the steps and ring on the hall door-bell, but he did not interest her.

"I shall find work to do," she said, "soon. I am grateful to you for—for taking me in, for giving me asylum here for a time—very, very grateful. I know that you meant well when you brought that man and me face to face last night—that man—" She paused.

She could see him now, that man with eager and earnest pleading in his eyes, with hands outstretched to her, as he told her of his love. And seeing him in memory, there came into her cheeks that flush that he had seen and remembered, and into her eyes the dewy, softness that banished all haughtiness, and made her for the moment the tender woman that she was.

"So," she said, "so I shall find work to do, and I will go out again and earn my living and—"

"There will be no need!" the General said.

"I cannot stop here and live on your charity!"

"There will be no need," he repeated.

"Mr. Rankin," announced a servant. The door had opened, and the man she had been watching came in.

He shook hands with the General.

"Joan, this is Mr. Rankin. Rankin, this is Miss Joan Meredyth."

She turned to him and bowed slightly.

"You will allow me to congratulate you, Miss Meredyth. Believe me, it is a great happiness to me that at last, after much diligent seeking, I have, thanks to the General here, found you. General—you have told her?" He broke off, for there was a puzzled look in the girl's face.

"Told her nothing—nothing," said the General; "that's your business."

Strangely, their words aroused little or no curiosity in her mind. What was it she had been told or not told, she did not know. Somehow she did not care. She saw a pair of pleading eyes, she saw the colour rise in a man's cheeks. She saw an outstretched hand, held pleadingly to her, and she had repulsed that hand in disdain.

But Mr. Rankin was talking.

"Your uncle, on his way back to this country, died on board ship. His only son was killed, poor fellow, in the War. There was no one else, the will leaves everything to you unconditionally. Through myself he had purchased the old place, Starden Hall, only a few months before his death, and it was his intention to live there. So the house and the money become yours, Miss Meredyth. There is Starden, and the income of roughly fifteen thousand a year, all unconditionally yours."

And listening, dazed for the moment, there came into her mind an unworthy thought—a thought that brought a sense of shame to her, yet the thought had come.

Did that man—last night—know of this, of this fortune when he had told her that he loved her?

A few days had passed, days that had found Joan fully

occupied with the many matters connected with her inheritance.

To-day she and the old General were talking in the drawing-room of the General's house.

"Of course, if you prefer it and wish it, my dear."

"I do!" said Joan. "I see no reason why Lady Linden should be in any way interested in me and my affairs. I prefer that you should tell her nothing at all. I was very fond of Marjorie, she is a dear little thing, and Lady Linden was very kind to me once, that is why I wrote to her. But now I would sooner forget it all. I shall go down to Starden and live."

"Alone?"

"I have no one, so I must be alone! Mr. Rankin says that all the business formalities will be completed this week, and there will be nothing to keep me. Mrs. Norton, the house-keeper at Starden, says the house is all ready, so I thought of going down at the beginning of next week!"

"Alone?" the old man repeated.

"Since I am alone, I must go alone."

"My dear, I am an old fellow, and likely to be in the way, but if—my society—would—"

Joan smiled, and the smile transfigured her. It brought tenderness and sweetness to the young face that adversity had somewhat hardened.

"No, I won't be selfish, dear," she said gently. "You would hate it; you are at home here, and you have all you want.

There you would be unhappy and uncomfortable; but I do thank you very, very gratefully."

"But you can't go alone, child. Why bless me, there's my niece Helen Everard. She's a widow, her husband's people live close to Starden at Buddesby. If only for a time, let me arrange with her to go with you."

"If you like," she said.

"I'll write to her at once," the General said, and Joan nodded, little dreaming what the sending of that letter might mean to her.

# CHAPTER XIV

## THE BEGINNING OF THE TRAIL

For a while the unrighteous may bask in the sunshine of prosperity, but there comes a time of reckoning, more especially in the City of London, and things were at this moment shaping ill for Mr. Philip Slotman.

He stood at the door of the general office and surveyed his clerks. There were five of them; at the end of the week there would be but two, he decided. Next week probably there would be only one.

"Hello, Slotman!" It was a business acquaintance, who had dropped in to discuss the financial position.

"Things all right?

"Nothing to complain about," said Slotman, who did not believe in crying stinking fish. Credit meant everything to him, and it was for that reason he wore very nice clothes and more jewellery than good taste warranted.

In Mr. Slotman's inner office he and his friend, Mr. James Bloomberg, lighted expensive cigars.

"So the pretty typist has gone, of course?" said Bloomberg.

Slotman started. "You mean—?"

"Miss Meredyth; I've heard about her."

"About her. What?"

Bloomberg drew at his cigar. "Of course you know she's come into money, a pot of money and a fine place down in the country. Uncle died, left a will—that sort of thing. Rankin acts for me, a sound man. I was talking to him the other day, and your name cropped up."

"Go on!" said Slotman. The cigar shook between, his finger and thumb. "My name cropped up?"

"And Rankin was interested, as a young lady he was acting for had just come into a pot of money and a fine place down in Kent, and he had heard that she used to be employed by you. Ah, ha!" Bloomberg laughed. "You oughtn't to have let her slip away, old man. She was as pretty as a peach, and now with some hundreds of thousands she will be worth while, eh?"

"I suppose so," Slotman said, apparently indifferently. "And did you hear the name of the place she had come into?"

"I did. Something—Den—all places in Kent are something or other—Den. Oh, Starden! That's it! Well, I must go. But tell me, what's your opinion about those Calbary Reef Preferentials?"

Ten minutes later Slotman was alone, frowning at thought. If it were true, then indeed the luck had been against him. Even without money he had been willing, more than willing to marry Joan, in spite of the past, of which he knew nothing, but suspected much. Yes, he would have married her.

"She got hold of me," he muttered, "and I can't leave off thinking of her, and now she is an heiress, and Heaven knows I want money. If I had a chance, if—" He paused.

For a long while Mr. Philip Slotman sat in deep thought. About Joan Meredyth there was a mystery, and it was a mystery that might be well worth solving.

"I'll hunt it out," he muttered. "I'll have to work back. Let me see, there was that old General—General—?"

He frowned, Ah! he had it now, for his memory was a good one.

"General Bartholomew! That was the name," Slotman muttered. "And that is where I commence my hunt!"

# CHAPTER XV

## "TO THE MANNER BORN"

Starden Hall was one of those half-timbered houses in the possession of which Kent and Sussex are rich. It was no great mansion, but a comfortable, rambling old house, that had been built many a generation ago, and had been added to as occasion required by thoughtful owners, who had always borne in mind the architecture and the atmosphere of the original, and so to-day it covered a vast quantity of ground, being but one storey high, and about it spread flower gardens and noble park-land that were delights to the eye.

And this place was hers. It belonged to her, the girl who a few short weeks ago had been earning three pounds a week in a City office, and whose nightmare had been worklessness and starvation.

Helen Everard watched the girl closely. "To the manner born," she thought. And yet there was that about Joan that she would have altered, a coldness, an aloofness. Too often the beautiful mouth was set and hard, never cruel, yet scornful. Too often those lustrous eyes looked coldly out on to a world that was surely smiling on her now.

"There's something—" the elder woman thought, for she was

Henry St. John Cooper

a clever and capable woman—a woman who could see under the surface of things, a woman who had loved and suffered, and had risen triumphant over misfortunes, which had been so many and so dire that they might have crushed a less valiant spirit.

General Bartholomew had explained briefly:

"The child is alone in the world. There is something I don't quite understand, Helen. It is about a marriage—" The old gentleman paused. "Look here, I'll tell you. I had a letter from Lady Linden, an old friend, and she begged me to find Joan and bring her and her young husband together again."

"Then she is married?"

"No, that is, I—I don't know. 'Pon my soul, I don't know—can't make head or tail of it! She says she isn't, and, by George! she isn't a girl who would lie; but if she isn't—well, I'm beaten, Helen. I can't make it out. At any rate, I did bring her and the lad, and a fine lad he is too, George Alston's son, together. And he left the house without seeing me, and afterwards the girl told me that he was practically a stranger to her, and that there had never been any marriage at all. At the same time she asked me not to write to Lady Linden, and she said that it was no business of hers, which was true, come to that. And so—so now she's come into this money, and she is utterly alone in the world, and wants to go to Starden to live—why, my dear—"

"I see," Helen said. "I shall be glad to go there for a time you know; it's Alfred's country."

"I remembered that."

"John Everard is living at Buddesby with his sister Constance.

They are two of the dearest people—the children, you know, of Alfred's brother Matthew."

"Yes—yes, to be sure," said the old gentleman, who was not in the slightest degree interested.

"And they will be nice for your Joan Meredyth to know," said Mrs. Everard.

"That's it, that's it! Take her about; let her see people, young people. Make her enjoy herself, and forget the past. I don't know what the past held. Joan is not one to make confidants; but I fancy that her past, poor child, has held more suffering than she cares to talk about. So try and make her forget it. Get the Everards over from Buddesby, or take her there; let her see people. But you know, you know, my dear. You're a capable woman!"

Yes, she was a capable woman, far more capable than even General Bartholomew realised. Clever and capable, kindly and generous of nature, and the girl interested her. It was only interest at first. Joan was not one to invite a warm affection in another woman at the outset. Her manner was too cold, too uninviting, and yet there was nothing repellent about it. It was as if, wounded by contact with the world, she had withdrawn behind her own defences. She, who had suffered insult and indignity, looked on all the world with suspicious, shy eyes.

"I will break down her reserve. I think she is lovable and sweet when once one can force her to throw aside this mask," Helen Everard thought.

So they had come to Starden together.

Joan had said little when she had first looked over the place;

Henry St. John Cooper

but Helen, watching her, saw a tinge of colour come into her cheeks, and her breast rise and fall quickly, which proved that Joan was by no means so unmoved as she would appear.

It was her home, the home of her people. It was to-day almost as it had been a hundred years ago, and a hundred years before that, and even a hundred years earlier still.

The low-pitched, old-fashioned rooms, with the mullioned windows, the deep embrasures, the great open, stone-slabbed hearths, with their andirons and dog-grates, the walls panelled with carved linen-fold oak, darkened by age alone and polished to a dull, glossy glow by hands that would work no more.

Through these rooms, each redolent of the past, each breathing of a kindly, comfortable home-life, the girl went, looking about her with eyes that saw everything and yet seemed to see nothing.

"You like it, dear?" Helen asked.

"It is all wonderful, beautiful!" Joan said, and yet she spoke with a touch of sadness in her voice.... "How—how lonely one might be here!" she added.

"You—you must not think of loneliness; you will never be lonely, my dear. If you are, it will be of your own choice!"

"Who knows?" Joan smiled sadly. She was thinking of a man who had told her that he loved her. There had been more than one, but the one man stood out clear and distinct from all others; she could even remember the words he had used.

"If, in telling you that I love you, I have sinned past all forgiveness, I glory in it, and I take not one word of it back."

Yet how could he love her? How could he, when he had insulted her, when he had used her name, as he had, when he had humiliated and shamed her, how could he profess to love her? And they had met but three times in their lives.

"Joan, dear," Helen Everard said, "Joan!"

"Yes? I am sorry, I—I was thinking." Joan looked up.

Helen had come into the room, an open letter in her hand.

"I wrote to John and Constance Everard, my nephew and niece," Helen said. "I told them I was here with you, and asked them to come over. They are coming to-morrow, dear. I think you will like them."

"I am sure I shall," Joan said; but there was no enthusiasm in her voice, only cold politeness that seemed to chill a little.

"I glory in it," she was thinking, "and take not one word of it back." She shrugged her shoulders disdainfully and turned away.

"What time will they be coming, Helen?" she asked, for she had made up her mind. She would think no more of this man, and remember no more of his speeches. She would wipe him out of her memory. Life for her would begin again here in Starden, and the past should hold nothing, nothing, nothing!

# CHAPTER XVI

## ELLICE

Buddesby, in the Parish of Little Langbourne, was a small place compared with Starden Hall. Buddesby claimed to be nothing more than a farmhouse of a rather exalted type. For generations the Everards had been gentlemen farmers, farming their own land and doing exceedingly badly by it.

Matthew, late owner of Buddesby, had taken up French gardening on a large scale, and had squandered a great part of his capital on glass cloches, fragments of which were likely to litter Buddesby for many a year to come.

John, his son, had turned his back on intensive culture and had gone back to the old family failing of hops. The Everard family had probably flung away more money on hops than any other family in Kent.

The Everards were not rich. The shabby, delightful old rooms, the tumble-down appearance of the ancient house, the lack of luxuries proved it, but they were exceedingly content.

Constance was a slim, pale, fair-haired girl with a singularly sweet expression and the temper, as her brother said often enough, of an angel. John Everard was big and broad, brown-haired, ruddy complexioned. He regarded every goose as a swan, and had unlimited belief in his land, his sister, and the future. There was one other occupant of Buddesby, a slight slender, dark-haired girl, with a thin, olive face, a pair of blazing black eyes, and a vividly red-lipped mouth.

Eight years ago Matthew Everard had brought her home after a brief visit to London. He had handed her over to eighteen-year-old Constance.

"Look after the little one, Connie," he had said. "There's not a soul in the world who wants her, poor little lass. Her father's been dead years; her mother died—last week." He paused. "I knew them both." That was all the information he had ever given, so Ellice Brand had come to Buddesby, one more mouth to feed, one more pair of feet to find shoes for.

She had many faults; she was passionate and wilful, defiant and impatient of even Connie's gentle authority. But there was one who could quell her most violent outburst with a word—one who had but to look at her to bring her to her sane senses, one whom she would, dog-like, have followed to the end of the world, from whom she would have accepted blows and kicks and curses without a murmur, only that Johnny Everard was not in the habit of bestowing blows and curses on young ladies.

Constance was twenty-six, John, the master of Buddesby, was a year younger, and Ellice was eighteen, her slender body as yet childish and unformed, her gipsy-like face a little too thin. But there was beauty there, wonderful and startling beauty that would one day blossom forth. It was in the bud as yet, but the bud was near to opening.

They were at breakfast in the comfortable, shabby old

morning-room at Buddesby. It was eight o'clock, and John had been afield for a couple of hours and had come back with his appetite sharp set.

They rose early at Buddesby. Constance had been at her housewifely duties since soon after six. Only Ellice had lain abed till the ringing of the breakfast-bell.

"A letter from Helen," Constance said.

"Helen? Oh, she's got to Starden then?" said John.

"And wants us to come over, dear."

"Of course! We'll go over next week some time. I'm busy now with—"

"It wouldn't be kind not to go at once."

"Who is Helen?" demanded Ellice. She looked fierce-eyed at Connie and then at John. "Who is she?" A tinge of colour came into her cheeks.

Connie saw it, and sighed a little. She knew this girl's secret, knew it only too well. Many an hour of anxiety and worry it had caused her.

"Helen is our aunt by marriage," she said.

"Oh!" Ellice said, "I thought—"

John laughed. He had a jolly laugh, a great hearty laugh that did one good to hear.

"What did you think she was, gipsy girl?" he asked, for "gipsy" was his pet name for the little dark beauty.

"Did you think she was some young and lovely damsel who was eager to meet me again?"

"I should hate her if she was!" the girl said, whereat John laughed again.

"Write to Helen, Con," he said as he rose from the table, "and say well come over to-morrow." He paused, frowning, at thought. "I'll manage it somehow. I'll drive you over in the trap. It would be useful to have a car; I don't know why I put off getting one."

Constance did, and she smiled. "Wait till next year, dear."

He nodded. "Yes, next year we'll get one. Meanwhile write to Helen, and tell her we'll be over to-morrow afternoon."

"And I?" Ellice asked.

John looked at her. "Why—no, child, you'll stop at home and look after the house, eh?" He nodded to them and went out.

"Is she there—alone?" Ellice asked.

"Who, dear?"

"This Helen, your aunt. Is it usual to call your aunt just plain Helen?"

"No, I suppose it isn't, and she is not there alone, as you ask. She is living with a girl who has just come into a great deal of money—Miss Joan Meredyth."

"What is she like?" the girl asked quickly.

Constance smiled.

"I don't know, dear. You see, I have never seen her."

"Then I hope," Ellice said between her clenched teeth, "I hope she is ugly, ugly as sin!"

"I think," said Constance gently, "that you are very silly and foolish!"

Yet when the morrow came it was Ellice and not Constance who sat beside John in the trap, and was driven by him the six odd miles to Starden. For Constance had one of "her headaches." It was no imaginary ailment, but a headache that prostrated her and filled her with pain, that made every sound an agony. She lay in her room, the blinds drawn, and all the household hushed.

"I'll write that we'll go to-morrow, dear," John said.

"No, go to-day. I should be glad, Johnny. Go to-day and take Ellice, I am so much better alone; and by the time you come home perhaps I shall have been able to sleep it off."

So Johnny Everard drove Ellice over to Starden that afternoon.

Helen Everard received them in the drawing-room. She was fond of Johnny Everard and his sister. This dark-faced girl she did not know, though she had heard of her. And now she looked at her with interest. It was an interesting face, such a face as one does not ordinarily see.

"One day, if she lives, she will be a beautiful woman," Helen thought. "To-day she is a gawky, passionate, ill-disciplined child; and I am afraid, terribly afraid, she is very much in love with that great, cheery, good-looking nephew of mine."

"Come," she said, "Joan is in the garden. I promised that when you came I would take you to her. You have heard about her of course?" Helen added to John.

"Only a little, that she is an heiress, and has come into Starden."

"She was very poor, poor child, and I think she had a hard and bitter time of it. Then the wheel of fortune took a turn. Her uncle died, and left her Starden and a great deal of money. So here she is."

Helen felt a hand grip her arm, and turned to look down into a thin face, in which burned a pair of passionate eyes.

"Is she—pretty?" the girl asked.

"I think," Helen said slowly, "that she is the most beautiful woman I have ever seen."

Unlike his usual self, John Everard was very silent and thoughtful as he drove home later that evening. Helen had said that Joan Meredyth was the most beautiful woman she had ever seen. He agreed with her whole-heartedly. She had received him and Ellice kindly, yet without much warmth, and now as he drove home in the light of the setting sun Johnny Everard was thinking about this girl, going over all that had happened, remembering every word almost that she had uttered.

"She is very beautiful, wonderfully beautiful," he thought. And perhaps he uttered his thoughts aloud, for the girl, as silent as himself, who sat beside him, started and looked up into his face, and into the passionate, rebellious heart of her there came a sudden wave of jealous hatred.

# CHAPTER XVII

## UNREST

Lady Linden patted the girl's small white hand.

"Yes, child," she said comfortably, "Colonel Arundel and I had a nice long talk last night, and you may guess what it was about. He and I were boy and girl together, there's no better blood in the kingdom than the Arundel's—what was I saying? Oh yes, we decided that it would be a good plan to have a two years' engagement, or better still, none for eighteen months, and then a six months' engagement. During that time Tom can study modern scientific farming and that sort of thing, you know, and then when you and he are married, he could take over these estates. I am heartily sick of Bilson, and I always fancy he is robbing me—what did you say, child?"

"Nothing, auntie."

"Well, you ought to be a very happy little girl. Run away."

But Marjorie lingered. "Aunt, you haven't heard anything of—of Hugh?" she asked.

"Hugh—Hugh Alston? Good gracious, no! You don't think I

am going to run after the man? I am disgusted with Hugh. His duplicity and, worse still, his obstinate, foolish, unreasoning behaviour, have annoyed me more than anything I ever remember. But there, my dear child, it is nothing to do with you. I have quite altered my opinion of Hugh Alston. You were right and I was wrong. Tom Arundel will make you a better husband, and you will be as happy as the day is long with him."

"I shan't!" Marjorie thought as she turned away. It was wrong, and it was unreasonable, and she knew it; but for the last four or five days there had been steadily growing in Marjorie's brain, an Idea.

Stolen fruits are sweetest, stolen meetings, moonlit assignations, shy kisses pressed on ardent young lips, when the world is shrouded in darkness and seems to hold but two. All these things make for romance. The silvery moonlight gives false values; the knowledge that one has slipped unseen from the house to meet the beloved one, and that the doing of it is a brave and bold adventure, gives a thrill that sets the heart throbbing and the young blood leaping—the knowledge that it is forbidden, and, being forbidden, very sweet, appeals to the young and romantic heart.

But when that same beloved object, looking less romantic in correct evening dress, is accepted smilingly by the powers that be, and is sate down to a large and varied, many coursed dinner, then Romance shrugs her disgusted shoulders and turns petulantly away.

It was so with Marjorie. When the idea first came to her, she felt shocked and amazed. It could not be! she said to herself. "I love Tom with all my heart and soul, and now I am the happiest girl living."

But she was not, and she knew it. It was useless to tell herself that she was the happiest girl living when night after night she lay awake, staring into the darkness and seeing in memory a face that certainly did not belong to Tom Arundel.

Hugh Alston had commenced work on the restoration of certain parts of Hurst Dormer. He had busied himself with the work, had entered whole-heartedly into all the plans, had counted up the cost, and then, realising that all his enthusiasm was only forced, that he was merely trying to cheat himself, he lost interest and gave it up.

"I'll go to London," he said. "I'll go and see things, and try and get thoughts of her out of my mind." So he went, and found London even more uninteresting than Hurst Dormer.

He had promised that he would never molest her, never annoy her with his visits or his presence, and he meant religiously to keep his word, and yet—if he could just see her! She need not know! If he could from a distance feast his eyes on her for one moment, on a sight of her, what harm would he do her or anyone?

Hugh Alston did not recognise himself in this restless dissatisfied, unhappy man, who took to loitering and wandering about the streets, haunting certain places and keeping a sharp lookout for someone who might or might not come.

So the days passed. He had gladdened his eyes three times with a view of old General Bartholomew. He had seen that ancient man leaning on his stick, taking a constitutional around the square.

And that was all! He passed the house and watched, yet saw no sign of her. He came at night-time, when tell-tale shadows might be thrown on the blinds, but saw nothing, only the shadow of the General or of his secretary, never one that might have been hers.

And then he slowly came to the conclusion that Joan Meredyth could no longer be there. It had taken him nearly a week to come to that decision.

That Joan had left General Bartholomew's house he was certain, but where was she? He had no right to enquire, no right to hunt her down. If he knew where she was, how could it profit him, for had he not promised to trouble her no more?

Yet still for all that he wanted to know, and casting about in his mind how he might find her, he thought of Mr. Philip Slotman.

It was possible that if she had left the General's she had gone back to take up her work with Slotman again.

"I'll risk it," he thought, and went to Gracebury and made his way to Slotman's office.

It was a sadly depleted staff that he found in the general office. An ancient man and a young boy represented Mr. Philip Slotman's one-time large clerical staff.

"Mr. Slotman's away, sir, down in the country—gone down to Sussex, sir," said the lad.

"To Sussex? Will he be away long?"

"Can't say, sir; he may be back to-morrow," the boy said. "At any rate, he's not here to-day."

"I may come back to-morrow. You might tell him that Mr.

Alston called." And Hugh turned away.

Another disappointment. He realised now that he had built up quite a lot of hope on his interview with Slotman.

"Shall I wait till to-morrow, or shall I go back to-day?" Hugh wondered. "This is getting awful. I don't seem to have a mind of my own, I can't settle down to a thing. I've got to get a grip on myself. How does the old poem go: 'If she be fair, but not fair to me, what care I how fair she be?' That's all right; but I do care, and I can't help it!"

He had made his aimless way back to the West End of London. It was luncheon time, and he was hesitating between a restaurant and an hotel.

"I'll go back to the hotel, get some lunch, pack up and leave by the five o'clock train for Hurst Dormer," he decided, and turned to hail a taxicab.

And, turning, he came suddenly face to face with the girl who was ever in his thoughts.

She had been helping a middle-aged, pleasant-faced woman out of a cab, and then, as she turned, their eyes met, and into Joan Meredyth's cheeks there flashed the tell-tale colour that proved to him and to all the world that this chance meeting with him meant something to her after all.

# CHAPTER XVIII

## "UNGENEROUS"

Hugh Alston had raised his hat, and she had given him the coolest of bows. He was turning away, true to his promise to trouble her no more, and her heart seemed to cry out against it suddenly.

If she could have believed that he had been here of deliberate intent, to find her, to see her, she would have felt cold anger against him; but it was an accident, and Joan knew suddenly that for some reason she was unwilling to let him go.

What she said she hardly knew, something about the unexpectedness of meetings that were common enough in London. At any rate she spoke, and was rewarded by the look that came into his face. A starving dog could not have looked more gratitude to one who had flung him a bone than Hugh Alston, starving for her, thanked her with his eyes for the few conventional words.

Before he could realise what had happened, she had introduced him to her companion.

"Helen, this is Mr. Alston—whom I—I know," she said.

Henry St. John Cooper

"Alston." Helen Everard congratulated herself afterwards that she had given no sign of surprise, no start, nothing to betray the fact that the name was familiar.

Here was the man then whom Lady Linden believed to be Joan's husband, the man whom Joan had denied she had married, and who she had stated to General Bartholomew was scarcely more than a stranger to her.

And, looking at him, Helen knew that if Hugh Alston and she met again, he would certainly not know her, for he had no eyes for anything save the lovely cold face of the girl before him.

"Oh, Joan," she said, "there is one of those bags I have been wanting to get for a long time past. Excuse me, Joan dear, will you?" And Helen made hurriedly to a shop hard by, leaving them together.

Joan felt angry with herself now it was too late. She ought to have given him the coldest of cold bows and then ignored him; but she had been weak, and she had spoken, and now Helen had deserted her.

"I will say good-bye, Mr. Alston, and go after my friend."

"No, wait—wait. I want to speak to you, to thank you."

"To thank me?" She lifted her eyebrows. "For what?"

"For speaking to me."

"That sounds very humble, doesn't it?" She laughed sharply.

"I am very humble to you, Joan!"

"Mr. Alston, do you realise that I am very angry with myself?" she said coldly. "I acted on a foolish impulse. I ought not to have spoken to you."

"You acted on a generous impulse, that is natural to you. Now you are pretending one that is unworthy of you, Joan."

"I do not think you have any right to speak to me so, nor call me by that name."

"I must call you by the name I constantly think of you by. Joan, do you remember what I said to you when we last met?"

"No, I—" She flushed suddenly. To deny, was unworthy of her. "Yes, I remember."

"It is true, remember what I said. I take not one word of it back. It is true, and will remain true all my life."

"My friend—will be wondering—"

"Joan, be a little merciful."

And now for the first time he noticed that she was not dressed as he had seen her last. There was a suggestion of wealth, of ample means about her appearance. Clothes were the last thing that Hugh thought of, or noticed. Yet gradually Joan's clothes began to thrust themselves on his notice. She was well dressed, and the stylish and becoming clothes heightened her beauty, if possible.

"Joan, I have a confession to make."

She bent her head.

"I couldn't act unfairly or deal in an underhand way with you."

"I thought differently!" she said bitterly.

"I remembered my promise made to you at General Bartholomew's, yet I came to London in the hope of seeing you, that was all that brought me here. I would not have spoken to you if you had not spoken to me first. I only wanted just to see you. I wonder," he went on, "that I have not been arrested as a suspicious character, as I have been loitering about General Bartholomew's house for days, but I never saw you, Joan!"

"I was not there!"

"No, I gathered that at last. You will believe that I had no intention of annoying you or forcing myself on your notice. I wanted to see you, that was all, and so when I had made up my mind that you were not there, I went to the City Office where I saw you last."

Her face flushed with anger.

"You have taken then to tracking me?" she said angrily.

"I am afraid it looks like it, but not to annoy you, only to satisfy my longing to see you. Just now you said I sounded humble. I wonder if you could guess how humble I feel."

"I wonder," she said sharply, "if you could guess how little I believe anything you say, Mr. Alston? I am sorry I spoke to you. It was a weakness I regret. Now I will say good-bye. You went to Slotman's office, and I suppose discussed me with him?"

"I did not; he was not there. I was glad afterwards he was not. I don't like the man."

"It does not matter. In any event Mr. Slotman could not have helped you; he does not know where I am living."

"Won't you tell me?"

"Why should I, to be further annoyed by you?"

"I think you know that I will not annoy you. Won't you tell me, Joan?"

"I—I don't see why I should. Remember, I have no wish to continue our—our acquaintance; there is no reason you should know."

"Yet if I knew I would be happier. I would not trouble you."

"Surely it does not matter. I am living in the country, then—in Kent, at Starden. I—I have come into a little money." She looked at him keenly. She wondered did he know, had he known that night when he had told her that he loved her?

"I am glad of it," he said. "I could have wished you had come into a great deal."

"I have!" she said quietly.

"I am truly glad," he said. "It was one of the things that troubled me most, the thought of you—you forced to go out into the world to earn your living, you who are so fine and exquisite and sensitive, being brought into contact with the ugly things of life. I am glad that you are saved that—it lightens my heart too, Joan."

"Why?"

"Haven't I told you? I hated the thought of you having to work for such a man as Slotman. I am thankful you are freed from any such need."

She had wronged him by that thought, she was glad to realise it. He had not known, then.

"My uncle died. He left me his fortune and the old home of our family, which he had recently bought back, Starden Hall, in Kent. I am living there now with Mrs. Everard, my friend and companion, and now—"

While she had been waiting to be served with a bag that she did not particularly require, Helen Everard watched them through the shop-window. She watched him particularly.

"I like him; he looks honest," she thought. "It is all strange and curious. If it were not true what Lady Linden said, why did she say it? If it is true, then—then why—what is the cause of the quarrel between them? Will they make it up? He does not look like a man who could treat a woman badly. Oh dear!" Helen sighed, for she had her own plans. Like every good woman, she was a born matchmaker at heart. She had a deep and sincere affection for John Everard. She had decided long ago that she must find Johnny a good wife, and here had been the very thing, only there was this Mr. Hugh Alston.

She had been served with the bag, it had been wrapped in paper for her, and now Helen came out. She had lingered as long as she could to give this man every chance.

"I am afraid I have been a long time, Joan," she began.

Hugh turned to her eagerly.

"Mrs.—Everard," he said, "I have been trying to induce Miss Meredyth to come and have lunch with me."

"Oh!" Joan cried. The word lunch had never passed his lips till now, and she looked at him angrily.

"I suggest Prince's," he said. "Let's get a taxi and go there now."

"Thank you, I do not require any lunch," Joan said.

"But I do, my dear. I am simply famished," said Helen.

It was like a base betrayal, but she felt that she must help this good-looking young man who looked at her so pleadingly.

"And it is always so much nicer to have a gentleman escort, isn't it?"

"You can't refuse now, Joan," Hugh said.

Joan! The name suggested to Helen that Joan had not spoken quite the truth when she had told General Bartholomew that she and this man were practically strangers. A strange man does not usually call a young girl by her Christian name.

"As you like," Joan said indifferently. She looked at Hugh resentfully.

"I do not consider it is either very clever or very considerate," she said in a low voice, intended for him alone.

"I am sorry, but—but I couldn't let you go yet. You—you don't understand, Joan!" he stammered.

She shrugged her shoulders; she went with them because she

must. She could not create a scene, but she would take her revenge. She promised herself that, and she did. She scarcely spoke a word during the luncheon. She ate nothing; she looked about her with an air of indifference. Twice she deliberately yawned behind her hand, hoping that he would notice; and he did, and it hurt him cruelly, as she hoped it might.

But she kept the worst sting for the last.

"Please," she said to the waiter, "make out the bills separately—mine and this lady's together, and the gentleman's by itself."

"Joan!" he said, as the waiter went his way, and his voice was shocked and hurt.

"Oh really, you could hardly expect that I would wish you to spend any of your—eight thousand a year on me!"

Hugh flushed. He bent his head. His eight thousand a year that once he had held out as a bait to her, and yet, Heaven knew, he had not meant it so. He had only meant to be frank with her.

He was hurt and stung, as she meant he should be, and seeing it, her heart misgave her, and she was sorry. But it was too late, and she must not confess weakness now.

There was a cold look in his face, a bitterness about his mouth she had never seen before. When he rose he held out his hand to Mrs. Everard; he thanked her for coming here with him, and then he gave Joan the coldest of cold bows. He held no hand out to her, he had no speech for her. Only one word, one word that once before he had flung at her, and now flung into her face again.

"Ungenerous!" he said, so that she alone could hear, and then he was gone, and Helen looked after him. And then, turning, she glanced at Joan, and saw that there were tears in the girl's grey eyes.

Henry St. John Cooper

# CHAPTER XIX

## THE INVESTIGATIONS OF MR. SLOTMAN

"And who the dickens," said Lady Linden, "is Mister—Philip what's-his-name? I can't see it—what's his name, Marjorie?" Lady Linden held out the card to the girl.

"It—it is—Slotman, auntie," Marjorie said.

"Don't sniff, child. You've got a cold; go up to my room, and in the medical—"

"I haven't a cold, auntie."

"Don't talk to me. Go and get a dose of ammoniated tincture of quinine. As for this Mr. Slotman—unpleasant name—what the dickens does he want of me?"

Marjorie did not answer.

Slotman was being shewn into the drawing-room a few moments later. He was wearing his best clothes and best manner. This Lady Linden was an aristocratic dame, and Mr. Slotman had come for the express purpose of making himself very agreeable.

"Oily-looking wretch!" her ladyship thought. "Well?" she asked aloud.

"I am grateful to your ladyship for permitting me to see you."

"Well, you can see me if that's all you have come for."

"No!" he said. "If—if I—" He paused.

"Oh, sit down!" said Lady Linden. "Well, now what is it you want? Have you something to sell? Books, sewing machines?"

"No, no!" He waved a deprecating hand. "I am come on a matter that interests me greatly. I am a financier, I have offices in London. Until lately I was employing a young lady on my staff."

"Well?"

"Her name was Meredyth, Miss Joan Meredyth."

"I don't want to hear anything at all about her," said Lady Linden. "Why you come to me, goodness only knows. If you've come for information I haven't got any. If you want information, the right person to go to is her husband!"

"Her—her husband!" Mr. Slotman seemed to be choking.

"You seem surprised," said Lady Linden. "Well, so was I, but it is the truth. If you are interested in Miss Meredyth, the proper person to make enquiries of is Mr. Hugh Alston, of Hurst Dormer, Sussex. Now you know. Is there anything else I can do for you?"

Slotman passed his hand across his forehead. This was

unexpected, a blow that staggered him.

"You—you mean, your ladyship means that Miss Meredyth is recently married."

"Her ladyship means nothing of the kind," said Lady Linden tartly. "I mean that Miss Meredyth has for some very considerable time been Mrs. Hugh Alston. They were married, if you want to know—and I don't see why it should any longer be kept a secret—three years ago, in June, nineteen eighteen at Marlbury, Dorset, where my niece was at school with Miss Meredyth. Now you know all I know, and if you want any further information, apply to the husband."

"But—but," Slotman said, "I—" He was thinking. He was trying to reconcile what he had heard in his own office when he had spied on Hugh Alston and Joan, when on that occasion he had heard Hugh offer marriage to the girl as an act of atonement. How could he offer marriage if they were already married? There was something wrong, some mistake!

"But what?" snapped her ladyship, who had taken an exceeding dislike to the perspiring Mr. Slotman.

"Is your ladyship certain that they were married? I mean—" he fumbled and stammered.

Lady Linden pointed to the door. "Good afternoon!" she said. "I don't know what business it is of yours, and I don't care. All I know is that if Hugh Alston is a fool, he is not a knave, so you have my permission to retire."

Mr. Slotman retired, but it was not till some hours had passed that he finally left the neighbourhood of Cornbridge.

He had been making discreet enquiries, and he found on every side that her ladyship's story was corroborated.

For Lady Linden talked, and it was asking too much of any lady who was fond of a chat to expect her to keep silent on a matter of such interest. Lady Linden had discussed Hugh Alston's marriage with Mrs. Pontifex, the Rector's wife, who in turn had discussed it with others. So, little by little, the story had leaked out, and all Cornbridge knew it, and Mr. Slotman found ample corroboration of Lady Linden's story.

Not till he was in the train did Mr. Slotman begin to gather together all the threads of evidence. "I should not describe Lady Linden as a pleasant person," he decided, "still, her information will prove of the utmost value to me. On the whole I am glad I went." He felt satisfied; he had discovered all that was discoverable, so far as Cornbridge was concerned.

"Married in eighteen, June of eighteen," he muttered, "at Marlbury, Dorset. I'll bet she wasn't! She may have said she was, but she wasn't!" He chuckled grimly. He was beginning to see through it. "I suppose she told that tale, and then it got about, and then the fellow came and offered her marriage as the only possible way out. I'd like to choke the brute!"

Slotman slept that night in London, and early the following morning he was on his way to Marlbury. He found it a little quiet country town, where information was to be had readily enough. It took him but a few minutes to discover that there was a school for young ladies, a school of repute, kept by a Miss Skinner. It was the only ladies' school in or near the town, and so Mr. Slotman made his way in that direction, and in a little time was ushered into the presence of the headmistress.

Henry St. John Cooper

"I must apologise," he said, "for this intrusion."

Miss Skinner bowed. She was tall and thin, angular and severe, a typical headmistress, stern and unyielding.

"I am," Slotman lied, "a solicitor from London, and I am interested in a young lady who a matter of three years ago was, I believe, a pupil in this school."

"Indeed?"

"Miss Joan Meredyth," said Slotman.

"Miss Meredyth was a pupil here at the time you mention, three years ago. It was three years ago that she left."

"In June?" Slotman asked.

"I think so. Is it important that you know?"

"Very!"

"I will go and look up my books." In a few minutes Miss Skinner was back.

"Miss Meredyth left us in the June of nineteen hundred and eighteen," she said.

"Suddenly?"

"Somewhat—yes, suddenly. Her father was dead; she was leaving us to go to Australia."

"So that was the story," Slotman thought, "to go to Australia."

"During the time she was here, may I ask, did she have any visitors? Did, for instance, a Mr. Hugh Alston call on her?"

"Mr. Alston, I remember the name. Certainly he called here, but not to see Miss Meredyth. He came to see Miss Marjorie Linden, who was, I fancy, distantly related to him. I am not sure, Mr. Alston certainly called several times."

"And saw Miss Meredyth?"

"I think not. I have no reason to believe that he did. Miss Linden and Miss Meredyth were close friends, and of course Miss Linden may have introduced him. It is quite possible."

"Thank you!" said Slotman. He had found out all that he wanted to know, yet not quite.

For the next few hours Philip Slotman was a busy man. He went to the church and looked up the register. No marriage such as he looked for had taken place between Hugh Alston and Joan Meredyth in June, nineteen eighteen, nor any other month immediately before or after. No marriage had taken place at the local Registrar's office. But he was not done yet. Six miles from Marlbury was Morchester, a far larger and more important town. Thither went Philip Slotman and pursued his enquiries with a like result.

Neither at Marlbury, nor at Morchester had any marriage been registered in the name of Hugh Alston and Joan Meredyth in the year nineteen eighteen; and having discovered that fact beyond doubt, Philip Slotman took train for London.

Henry St. John Cooper

# CHAPTER XX

## "WHEN I AM NOT WITH YOU"

A fortnight had passed since Johnny Everard's first visit to Starden, and during that time he had been again and yet again. He had never taken Ellice with him since that first time.

Two days after the first visit he had driven Constance over, and Constance and Joan Meredyth had become instant friends.

"You'll come again and often; it is lonely here," Joan had said. "I mean, not lonely for me, that would be ungrateful to Helen, but I know she is very fond of you, and she will like you to come as often as possible, you and your brother."

"Con," Johnny said as he drove her home that evening, "don't you think we might run to a little car, just a cheap two-seater? It would be so useful. Look, we could run over to Starden in less than half an hour. We can be there and back in an hour if we wanted to, and Helen would be so jolly glad, don't you think?"

Constance smiled to herself.

"We haven't much money now, Johnny," she said. "Last year's hops were—awful!"

"They are going to be ripping this year. I've got that blight down all right," he said cheerily.

"Yes, dear; well, if you think—" She hesitated.

"Oh, we can manage it somehow," he said hopefully.

Constance looked at him out of the corner of her eyes.

"It will be useful for you to run over to Starden to see Helen—won't it?"

"Yes, to see Helen. She's a good sort, one of the best, dear old Helen! Isn't it ripping to have her near us again?"

"She could always have come to Buddesby if she had wanted to."

"Oh, there isn't much room there!"

"But always room enough for Helen, Johnny. You haven't told me what you think of Joan Meredyth."

She watched him out of the corners of her eyes. He stared straight ahead between the ears of the old horse.

"Joan Meredyth," he repeated, and she saw a deep flush come stealing under the tan of his cheeks. "Oh, she's handsome, Con. She almost took my breath away. I think she is the loveliest girl I ever saw."

"Yes, and do you—"

"And do I admire her? Yes, I do, but I could wish she was just a little less cold, a little less stately, Con."

"Perhaps it is shyness. Remember, we are strangers to her; she was not cold and stately to me, Johnny."

"Ah!" Johnny said, and went on staring straight ahead down the road.

"Did Helen say much to you, Con?"

"Oh, a good deal!"

"About"—Johnny hesitated—"her?"

"Yes, a little; she thinks a great deal of her. She says that at first Joan seemed to hold her at arm's length. Now they understand one another better, and she says Joan has the best heart in the world."

"Yet she seems cold to me," said Johnny with a sigh.

Still, in spite of Joan's coldness, he found his way over to Starden very often during the days that followed. He had picked up a small secondhand car, which he strenuously learned to drive, and thereafter the little car might have been seen plugging almost daily along the six odd miles of road that separated Buddesby from Starden.

And each time he got the car out a pair of black eyes watched him with smouldering anger and passion and jealousy. A pair of small hands were clenched tightly, a girl's heart was aching and throbbing with love and hate and undisciplined passions, as though it must break.

But he did not see, though Constance did, and she felt

troubled and anxious. She had understood for long how it was with Ellice. She had seen the girl's eyes turned with dog-like devotion towards the man who was all unconscious of the passion he had aroused. But she saw it all in her quiet way, and was anxious and worried, as a kindly, gentle, tender-hearted woman must be when she notices one of her own sex give all the love of a passionate heart to one who neither realises nor desires it.

So, day after day, Johnny drove over to Starden, and when he came Helen would smile quietly and take herself off about some household duty, leaving the young people together. And Joan would greet him with a smile from which all coldness now had gone, for she accepted him as a friend. She saw his sterling worth, his honour and his honesty. He was like some great boy, so open and transparent was he. To her he had become "Johnny," to him she was "Joan."

To-day they were wandering up and down the garden paths, side by side.

The garden lay about them, glowing in the sunshine of the early afternoon. Beyond the high bank of hollyhocks and the further hedge of dark yew, clipped into fantastic form, one could catch a glimpse of the old house, with its steep sloping roof, its many gables, its whitened walls, lined and crossed by the old timbers. The hum of the bees was in the air, heavy with the fragrance of many flowers.

And Joan was thinking of a City office, of a man she hated and feared, a man with bold eyes and thick, sensual lips. And then her thoughts drifted away to another man, and she seemed to hear again the last word he had spoken to her— "Ungenerous." And suddenly she shivered a little in the warm sunlight.

"Joan, you are not cold. You can't be cold," Johnny said.

She laughed. "No, I was only thinking of the past. There is much in the past to make one shiver, I think, and oh, Johnny, I was thinking of you too!"

"Of me?"

She nodded. "Helen was telling me how keen and eager you were about your farm, how difficult it was to get you to leave it for an hour." She paused. "That—that was before you came here, the first time—and since then you have been here almost every day. Johnny, aren't you wasting your time?" She looked at him with sweet seriousness.

"I am wasting my time, Joan, when—when I am not with you!" he said, and his voice shook with sudden feeling, and into his face there came a wave of colour. "To be near you, to see you—" He paused.

Down the garden pathway came a trim maidservant, who could never guess how John Everard hated her for at least one moment of her life.

"A gentleman in the drawing-room, miss, to see you," the girl said.

"A gentleman to see me? Who?"

"He would not give a name, miss. He said you might not recognise it. He wishes to see you on business." Joan frowned. Who could it be? Yet it was someone waiting, someone here.

"I shall not be long," she said to Johnny, and perhaps was glad of the excuse to leave him.

"I will wait till you come back, Joan."

She smiled and nodded, and hastened to the house and the drawing-room, and, opening the door, went in to find herself face to face with Philip Slotman.

* * * * *

Philip Slotman, of all living people! She stared at him in amaze, almost doubting the evidence of her sight. What did he here? How dared he come here and thrust himself on her notice? How dared he send that lying message by the maid, that she might not recognise his name?

"You've got a nice place here, Joan," he said with easy familiarity. "Things have looked up a bit for you, eh? I notice you haven't said you are glad to see me. Aren't you going to shake hands?"

"Explain," she said quietly, "what you mean by coming here."

If she had given way to senseless rage, and had demanded how he dared—and so forth, he would have smiled with amusement; but the cool deliberation of her, the quiet scorn in her eyes, the lack of passion, made him nervous and a little uncomfortable.

"I came here to see you—what else, Joan?"

"Uninvited," she said. "You have taken a liberty—"

"Oh, you!" he shouted suddenly. "You're a fine one to ride the high horse with me! Who the dickens are you to give yourself airs? You can stow that, do you hear?" His eyes flashed unpleasantly. "You can stow that kind of talk with me!"

"You came here believing, I suppose, that I was practically friendless. You knew that I had no relatives, especially men relatives, so you thought you would come to continue your annoyance of me. Would you mind coming here?"

He went to the window wonderingly. The window commanded a wide view of the garden. Looking out into the garden he could see a man, a very tall and very broad young man, who stood with muscular arms folded across a great chest. The young man was leaning against an old rose-red brick wall, smoking a pipe and obviously waiting. The most noticeable thing about the young man was that he was exceptionally big and of powerful build and determined appearance. Another thing that Slotman noticed about him was that he was not Mr. Hugh Alston, whom he remembered perfectly.

"Well?"

"That gentleman is a friend of mine, related to the lady who lives with me. If I call on him and ask him to persuade you to go and not return, he will do so."

"Oh, he will, and what then?"

"I don't understand you—what then? Why did you come here uninvited? Why did you send an untruthful message by my servant—that I would not recognise your name?"

"Trying to bluff me, aren't you?" Slotman said. He looked her in the eyes. "But it won't come off, Joan; no, my dear, I've been too busy of late to be taken in by your airs and defiance!" He laughed. "I've been making quite a round, here, there, and everywhere, and all because of you, Joan— all because of you! Among other places I've been to," he went on, seeing that she stood silent and unmoved, "is

Marlbury You remember it, eh? A nice little town, quiet though. I had a long talk with Miss Skinner—remember her, don't you, Joany?"

Her eyes glittered. "Mr. Slotman, I am trying to understand what this means. Is it that you are mad or intoxicated? Why do you come here to me with all these statements? Why do you come here at all?"

"Marlbury," he continued unmoved, "a nice, quiet little place. I spent some time in the church there, and at the Council offices, looking for something, for something I didn't find, Joany—and didn't expect to find either, come to that, ha, ha!" He laughed. "No, never expected to find, but, to make dead sure, I went to Morchester, and hunted there, Joany, and still I didn't find what I was looking for and knew I shouldn't find!"

"Mr. Slotman!"

"You aren't curious, are you? You won't ask what I was looking for, perhaps you can guess!" He took a step nearer to her. "You can guess, can't you, Joany?" he said.

"I am not attempting to guess. I can only imagine that you are not in your sane senses. You will now go, and if you return—"

"Wait a moment. What I was looking for at Marlbury and Morchester and did not find—was evidence of a marriage having taken place in June, nineteen eighteen, between Hugh Alston and Joan Meredyth. But there's no such evidence, none! Ah, that touches you a bit, don't it? Now you begin to understand why I ain't taken in by your fine dignity!"

"You—you have been looking for—for evidence of a

Henry St. John Cooper

marriage—my marriage with—what do you mean?"

Her face was flushed, her eyes brilliant with anger.

"I mean that I am not a fool, though I was for a time. You took me in—I am not blaming you"—he paused—"not blaming you. You were only a girl, straight out of school. You didn't understand things, and the man—"

"What—do—you—mean?" she whispered.

"You left Miss Skinner's, said you were going to Australia, didn't you? But you didn't go. Oh no, you didn't go! You know best where you went, but there's no proof of any marriage at Marlbury or Morchester. Now—now do you begin to understand?"

She did understand, a sense of horror came to her, horror and shame that this man should dare—dare to think evil of her! She felt that she wanted to strike him. She saw him as through a mist—his hateful face, the face she wanted to strike with all her might, and yet she was conscious of an even greater anger, a very passion of hate and resentment against another man than this, against the man who had subjected her to these insults, this infamy. She gripped her hands hard.

"You—you will leave this house. If you ever dare to return I will have you flung out—you hear me? Go, and if you ever dare—"

"No, no you don't!" he said. "Wait a moment. You can't take me in now!" He laughed in her face. "If I go I'll go all right, but you'll never hear the end of it. You're someone down here, aren't you? I have heard about you. You're a Meredyth, and the Meredyths used to hold their heads pretty high about here. But if you aren't careful I'll get talking, and if I talk I'll make this place too hot to hold you. You know what I mean. I hate threatening you, Joan, only you force me to do it." His voice altered. "I hate threatening, and you know why. It is because I love you, and I am willing to marry you—in spite of everything, you understand? In spite of everything!"

Joan threw out her hand and grasped at the edge of the table.

"My friend out there—am I to call for him? Are you driving me to do that? Shall I call him now?"

"If you like," Slotman said. "If you do, I'll have something to tell him of a marriage that never took place in June, nineteen eighteen, and of a man who came to my office to see you, and offered to marry you—as atonement. Oh yes, I heard— trust me! I don't let interviews take place in my offices that I don't know anything about!"

He was silent suddenly. There was that in her face that worried him, frightened him in spite of himself—a wild, staring look in her eyes; the whiteness of her cheeks, the whiteness even of her lips. There was a tragic look about her. He had seen something like it on the stage at some time. He realised that he might be goading her too far.

"I'll go now," he said. "I'll go and leave you to think it all out. You can rely on me not to say anything. I shan't humble you, or talk about you—not me! A man don't run down the girl he means to make his wife, and that's what I mean— Joan! In spite of everything, you understand, my girl?" He paused. "In spite of everything, Joan, I'll still marry you! But I'll come back. Oh, I'll come back, I—" He paused. He suddenly remembered the denuded state of his finances, yet it did not seem an auspicious moment just now to ask her for financial help.

"I'll write," he thought. He looked at her.

"Good-bye, Joan. I'll come back; you'll hear from me soon. Meanwhile, remember—not a word, not a word to a living soul. You're all right, trust me!"

Meanwhile Johnny Everard wandered about the sweet, old-world garden, and did not appreciate its beauties in the least. He was waiting, and there is nothing so dreary as waiting for one one longs to see and who comes not.

But presently there came a maid, that same maid who had earned Johnny's temporary hatred.

"Miss Meredyth wished me to say, sir, that she would be very glad if you would excuse her. She's been taken with a bad headache, and has had to go to her own room to lie down."

"Oh!" said Johnny. The sun seemed to shine less brightly for him for a few moments. "I'm sorry. All right, tell her I am very sorry, and—and shall hope to see her soon!"

Ten minutes later Johnny Everard was driving back along the hot high-road, utterly unconscious that the car was running very badly and misfiring consistently.

In her own room Joan sat, her elbows on the dressing-table, her eyes staring unseeingly out into a garden, all glowing with flowers and sunlight.

She was not thinking of Johnny Everard; his very existence had for the time being passed from her memory. She was thinking of that man, and of what he had said, the horror and the shame of it. And that other man—Hugh Alston—had brought this upon her—with his insulting lie, his insolent, lying statement, he had brought it on her! Because of him she was to be subjected to the shame and humiliation of such an attack as Slotman had made on her just now.

"Oh, what—what can I do?" she whispered. "And he—he dared to call me—me ungenerous! Ungenerous for resenting, for hating him for the position he has put me into. Why did he do it? Why, why, why?" she asked of herself frantically, and receiving no answer, rose and for a time paced the room, then came back to the table and sat down once again.

Slotman had said he would return, that she would hear. She could imagine how that the man, believing her good name in his power, and at his mercy, would not cease to torment and persecute her.

What could she do? To whom could she turn? She thought of Johnny Everard for a fleeting moment. There was something so big and strong and honest about him that he reminded her of some great, noble, clean dog, yet she could not appeal to him. Had he been her brother—that would have been different—but how explain to him? No, she could not. Yet she must have protection from this man, this Slotman. Lady Linden, General Bartholomew, Helen Everard, name after name came into her mind, and she dismissed each as it came. To whom could she turn? And then came the idea on which she acted at once. Of course it must be he!

She rose and sought for pen and paper, and commenced a letter that was difficult to write. She crushed several sheets of paper and flung them aside, but the letter was written at last.

"Because you have placed me in an intolerable position, and have subjected me to insult and annoyance past all bearing, I ask you to meet me in London at the earliest opportunity. I feel that I have a right to appeal to you for some protection against the insults to which your conduct has exposed me. I write in the hope that you may possibly possess some of the generosity which you have several times denied that I can lay claim to. I will keep whatever appointment you may make at any time and any place,

"JOAN MEREDYTH."

And this letter she addressed to Hugh Alston at Hurst Dormer, and presently went out, bareheaded, into the roadway, and with her own hands dropped it into the post-box.

# CHAPTER XXI

## "I SHALL FORGET HER"

Restless and unhappy, Hugh Alston had returned to Hurst Dormer, to find there that everything was flat, stale, and unprofitable. He had an intense love for the home of his birth and his boyhood, but just now it seemed to mean less to him than it ever had before. He watched moodily the workmen at their work on those alterations and restorations that he had been planning with interested enthusiasm for many months past. Now he did not seem to care whether they were done or no.

"Why," he demanded of the vision of her that came to him of nights, "why the dickens don't you leave me alone? I don't want you. I don't want to remember you. I am content to forget that I ever saw you, and I wish to Heaven you would leave me alone!"

But she was always there.

He tried to reason with himself; he attempted to analyse Love.

"One cannot love a thing," he told himself, "unless one has every reason to believe that it is perfection. A man, when he is deeply in love with a woman, must regard her as his ideal of womanhood. In his eyes she must be perfection; she must be flawless, even her faults he will not recognise as faults, but as perfections that are perhaps a little beyond his understanding—that's all right. Now in the case of Joan, I see in her nothing to admire beyond the loveliness of her face, the grace of her, the sweet voice of her and—oh, her whole personality! But I know her to be mean-spirited and uncharitable, unforgiving, ungenerous. I know her to be all these, and yet—"

"Lady Linden, sir, and Miss Marjorie Linden!"

They had not met for weeks. Her ladyship had driven over in the large, comfortable carriage. "Give me a horse or, better still, two horses—things with brains, created by the Almighty, and not a thing that goes piff, piff, piff, and leaves an ungodly smell along the roads, to say nothing of the dust!"

So she had come here behind two fine horses, sleek and overfed.

"Hello!" she said.

"Hello!" said Hugh, and kissed her, and so the feud between them was ended.

"You are looking," her ladyship said, "rotten!"

"I am looking exactly as I feel. How are you, Marjorie?" He held the small hand in his, and looked kindly, as he must ever look, into her pretty round face. Because she was blushing with the joy of seeing him, and because her eyes were bright as twin stars, he concluded that she was happy, and ascribed her happiness, not unnaturally considering everything, to Tom Arundel.

"As the cat," said Lady Linden, "wouldn't go to Mahomed—"

"The mountain, you mean!" Hugh said.

"Oh, I don't know. I knew it was a cat, a mountain or a coffin that one usually associates with Mahomed. However, as you didn't come, I came—to see what on earth you were doing, shutting yourself up here in Hurst Dormer."

"Renovations."

"They don't agree with you. I expect it's the drains. You're doing something to the drains, aren't you?"

"Yes, I believe—"

"Then go and get a suitcase packed, and come back with us to Cornbridge."

He would not hear of it at first; but Lady Linden had made up her mind, and she was a masterful woman.

"You'll come?"

"Really, I think I had better—not. You see—"

"I don't see! Marjorie, go out into the garden and smell the flowers. Keep away from the drains.... You'll come?" she repeated, when the girl had gone out.

"Look here, I know what is in your mind; if I come, it will be on one condition!" Hugh said.

"I know what that condition is. Very well, I agree; we won't mention it. Come for a week; it will do you good. You're too young to pretend you are a hermit!"

"You'll keep that condition; a certain name is not to be mentioned!"

"I am no longer interested in the—young woman. I shall certainly not mention her name. I think the whole affair—However, it is no business of mine, I never interfere in other people's affairs!" said Lady Linden, who never did anything else.

"All right then, on that condition I'll come, and it is good of you to ask me!"

"Rot!"

Hugh sent for his housekeeper.

"I am going to Cornbridge for a few days. I'll leave you as usual to look after everything. If any letters—come—there will be nothing of importance, I may run over in a couple of days to see how things are going on. Put my letters aside, they can wait."

"Very good, sir!" said Mrs. Morrisey. And the first letter that she carefully put aside was the one that Joan Meredyth had written, after much hesitation and searching of mind, in her bedroom that afternoon at Starden.

And during the days that followed Joan watched the post every morning, eagerly scanned the few letters that came, and then her face hardened a little, the curves of her perfect lips straightened out.

She had made a mistake; she had ascribed generosity and

decency to one who possessed neither. He had not even the courtesy to answer her letter, in which she had pleaded for a meeting. She felt hot with shame of herself that she had ever stooped to ask for it. She might have guessed.

A week had passed since Slotman's visit, and since she had with her own hands posted the letter to Hugh Alston. A week of waiting, and nothing had come of it! This morning she glanced through the letters. Her eyes had lost their old eagerness; she no longer expected anything.

As usual, there was nothing from "Him," but there was one for her in a handwriting that she knew only too well. She touched it as if it were some foul thing. She was in two minds whether to open and read it, or merely return it unopened and addressed to Philip Slotman, Esq., Gracebury, London, E.C. But she was a woman. And it takes a considerable amount of strength of will to return unopened and unread a letter to its sender, especially if one is a woman.

What might not that letter contain? Apology—retraction, sorrow for the past, or further insolent demands, veiled threats, and a repetition of proposals refused with scorn and contempt—which was it? Who can tell by the mere appearance of a sealed envelope and the impress of a postmark?

Joan put the letter into her pocket. She would debate in her mind whether she would read it or no.

"A letter from Connie, dear," said Helen. "She is coming over this afternoon and bringing Ellice Brand with her. Joan, it is a week or more since Johnny was here."

"Yes, about a week I think," said Joan indifferently. She was thinking meanwhile of the letter in her pocket.

Helen looked at her. She wanted to put questions; but, being a sensible woman, she did not. She had a great affection for Johnny. What woman could avoid having an affection and a regard for him? He was one of those fine, clean things that men and women, too, must like if they are themselves possessed of decency and appreciation of the good.

Yes, she was fond of Johnny, and she had grown very fond of late of this girl. She looked under the somewhat cold surface, and she recognised a warm, a tender and a loving nature, that had been suppressed for lack of something on which to lavish that wealth of tenderness that she held stored up in her heart.

Quite what part Hugh Alston had played in the life of Joan, Helen did not know. But she hoped for Johnny. She wanted to see these two come together. She was not above worldly considerations, for few good women are. It would be a fine thing for Johnny, with his straitened income and his habit of backing losers—from an agricultural point of view; but the main thing, as she honestly believed, was that these two could be very happy together. So she wondered a little, and puzzled a little, and worried a little why Johnny Everard should suddenly have left off paying almost daily visits to Starden.

"I like Connie, and I shall be glad to see her," said Joan.

"I wish Johnny were coming instead of—"

"So do I!" said Joan heartily. "I like him, I think, even more than I like Connie. There is something so—so honest and straight and good about him. Something that makes one feel, 'Here is a man to rely on, a man one can ask for help when in distress.' Sometimes—" She paused, then suddenly she rose, and with a smile to Helen, went out.

So there had been no quarrel, why should there have been? Certainly there had not been. Joan had spoken handsomely of Johnny, and she had said only what was true.

"I shall tell Connie exactly what Joan said, and probably Connie will repeat it to Johnny," Helen thought, which was exactly what she wished Connie would do.

In her own room Joan hesitated a moment, then tore open the envelope, and drew out Mr. Philip Slotman's letter.

"MY DEAR JOAN (her eyes flashed at the insolent familiarity of it). Since my visit of a week ago, when you received me so charmingly, I have constantly thought of you and your beautiful home, and you cannot guess how pleased I am to feel that the wheel of fortune had taken a turn to lift you high above all want and poverty."

She went on reading steadily, her lips compressed, her face hard and bitter.

"Unfortunately of late, things have not gone well with me. It is almost as if, when you went, you took my luck away with you. At any rate, I find myself in the immediate need of money, and to whom should I appeal for a timely loan, if not to one between whom and myself there has always been warm affection and friendship, to say the least of it? That I am in your confidence, that I know so much of the past, and that you trust in me so completely to respect all your secrets, is a source of pleasure and pride to me. So knowing that we do not stand to one another in the light of mere ordinary friends, I do not hesitate to explain my present embarrassment to you, and ask you frankly for the loan of three thousand pounds, which will relieve the most pressing of my immediate liabilities. Secure in the knowledge that you will immediately come to my aid, as

Henry St. John Cooper

you know full well I would have come to yours, had the positions been reversed, I am, my dear Joan,

"Yours very affectionately,
"PHILIP SLOTMAN."

The letter dropped from her hands to the carpet. Blackmail! Cunningly and cleverly wrapped up, but blackmail all the same, the reference to his knowledge of what he believed to be her past! He knew that she was one who would read and understand, that she would read, as is said, between the lines.

Three thousand pounds, to her a few short weeks ago a fortune; to her now, a mere row of figures. She could spare the money. It meant no hardship, no difficulty, and yet—how could she bring herself to pay money to the man?

She would not do it. She would return the letter, she would write across it some indignant refusal, and then—No, she would think it over, take time, consider. She was strong, and she was brave—she had faced an unkindly world without losing heart or courage. Yet this was an experience new to her. She was, after all, only a woman, and this man was assailing that thing which a woman prizes beyond all else— her good name, her reputation, and she knew full well how he might circulate a lying story that she would have the utmost difficulty in disproving now. He could fling mud, and some of it must stick!

Charge a person with wrongdoing, and even though it be definitely proved that he is innocent, yet people only remember the charge, the connection of the man's name with some infamy, and forget that he was as guiltless as they themselves.

Joan knew this. She dreaded it; she shuddered at the thought that a breath should sully her good name. She was someone now—a Meredyth—the Meredyth of Starden. Three thousand pounds! If she paid him for his silence—silence— of what, about what? Yet his lies might—She paced the room, her brain in a whirl. What could she do? Oh, that she had someone to turn to. She remembered the unanswered letter she had sent to Hugh Alston, and then her eyes flashed, and her breast heaved.

"I think," she said, "I think of the two I despise him the more. I loathe and despise him the more!"

# CHAPTER XXII

## JEALOUSY

Joan and Constance Everard had taken a natural and instinctive liking for one another. But to-day it seemed to Connie that Joan was silent, less friendly, more thoughtful than usual. Her mind seemed to be wondering, wrestling perhaps with some problem, of which Constance knew nothing, and so it was.

"What shall I do? Shall I send this man the money he demands, or shall I refuse? And if I refuse, what then?"

She knew that mud sticks, and she dreaded it, feared it. A threat of bodily pain she could have borne with a smile of equanimity, but this was different. She was so sensitive, so fine, so delicate, that the thought of scandal, of lies that might besmirch her, filled her with fear and shame and dread. It was weak perhaps, it was perhaps not in accord with her high courage, and yet frankly she was afraid.

"I shall send the money." She came to the decision suddenly. Connie was speaking to her, about her brother, Joan believed, yet was not certain. Her thoughts were far away with Slotman and his letter and his demand.

"I shall send the money." And having made up her mind, she felt instant relief. Yes, cowardly it might be, yet would it not be wiser to silence the man, to pay him this money that she might have peace, that scandal and shame might not touch her?

"I wanted him to come with us this afternoon, but he could not. It is the hops!" Connie sighed. "You don't know what a constant dread and worry hops can be, Joan. There is always the spraying. Johnny is spraying hard now. Of course we are not rich, and a really bad hop season is a serious thing."

"Of course!" Joan said. Yes, she would send the money. She would send the man a cheque this very day, as soon as the visitors were gone.

"I think she is worried about something," Connie thought. "It cannot be that she and Johnny have had a disagreement, yet for the last week he has been worried, different—so silent, so quiet, so unlike himself. I wonder—?"

She had brought the dark-eyed slip of a girl with her to-day, and from a distance Ellice sat watching the girl whom she told herself she hated—this girl who had in some strange way affected and bewitched Johnny, Johnny who belonged to her, Johnny whom she loved with a passionate devotion only she herself could know the depth of. How she hated her, she thought, as she sat watching the calm, beautiful, thoughtful face, with its strange, dreamy, far-away look in the big grey eyes.

She realised her beauty; she could not blind herself to it. She felt she must admire it because it was so apparent, so glowing, so obtrusive; and because she did admire it, she felt that she hated the owner of it the more.

　　　　　Henry St. John Cooper

"Why can't she leave Johnny alone? I've known him all these years, and it seems as if he had belonged to me. He never looked at any other girl, and now—now—she is here with all her money and her looks—and he is bewitched, he is different."

Helen rose; she wanted a few quiet words with Connie.

"I want to show you something in the garden, Connie," she said. "I know Joan won't mind." And so the two went out and left Joan alone with the girl, who watched her silently.

Out in the garden Helen and Constance had what women love and hold so dear—a heart-to-heart talk, an exchange of secrets and ideas.

"Do you think she cares for him?"

"I don't know, dear; but do you think he cares for her?"

"I am certain of it!"

"She spoke of him very nicely to-day. She said—" Helen repeated Joan's exact words.

So they talked, these two in the garden, of their hopes and of what might be, unselfish talk of happiness that might possibly come to those they loved, and in the drawing-room Ellice Brand eyed this girl, her rival, whom she hated.

"Will you excuse me?" Joan said suddenly. "There is a letter I must write. I have just remembered that the post goes at five, so—"

"Of course!"

She laughed sharply when Joan had gone out. "If he were here, it would be different. She would be all smiles and graciousness, but I am not worth while bothering about."

Joan wrote the cheque. It was for a large sum, the largest cheque not only that she had ever drawn, but that she had ever seen in her life. But it would be money well spent; it would silence the slanderous tongue.

"I am sending you the money you demand. I understand your letter thoroughly. I am neither going to defend myself, nor excuse myself to you. I of course realise that I am paying blackmail, and do so rather than be annoyed and tormented by you. Here is your money. I trust I shall neither hear of you nor see you again.

"JOAN MEREDYTH."

And this letter Joan posted with her own hand in the same post-box into which she had dropped that letter more than a week ago, the letter to a man who was without chivalry and generosity. She thought of him at the moment she let this other letter fall.

Yes, of the two she despised him and hated him the more.

And then when the letter was posted and gone beyond recall, again came the self-questionings. Had she done right? Had she not acted foolishly and weakly, to pay this man money that he had demanded with covert threats? And too late she regretted, and would have had the letter back if she could.

"I have no one, not a soul in the world I can turn to. Even Helen is almost a stranger," the girl thought. "I cannot confide in her. I seem to be so—so alone, so utterly alone." She twisted her hands together and stood thoughtful for some moments in the roadway where she turned back through the garden gate to the house.

"I feel so—so tired," she whispered, "so tired, so weary of it all. I have no one to turn to."

# CHAPTER XXIII

## "UNCERTAIN—COY"

Mr. Tom Arundel, cheerful and happy-go-lucky, filled with an immense belief in a future which he was sure would somehow shape itself satisfactorily, felt a little hurt, a little surprised, just a little disenchanted.

"I can't think what's come over her. She used to be such a ripping little thing, so sweet and good-tempered, and now— why she snaps a chap's head off the moment he opens his mouth. Goo-law!" said Tom. "Supposing she grows up to be like her aunt—maybe it is in the blood!"

The prospect seemed to overwhelm him for a moment. Certainly of late Marjorie had been uncertain, coy, and very hard to please. Marjorie had suffered, and was suffering. She was contrasting Tom with Hugh, and Hugh with Tom, and it made her heart ache and made her angry with herself for her own previous blindness. And, womanlike, being in a very bad temper with herself, she snapped at the luckless Tom like an ill-conditioned terrier, and he never approached her but that she, metaphorically, bared her pretty white teeth, ready to do battle with him.

"Rum things, girls—never know how to take 'em! She don't

seem like the same," thought Tom. "I wonder—"

There had been a breeze, a distinct breeze. Perhaps Tom, anxious to propitiate Lady Linden, had been a little more servile than usual. He did not mean to be servile. Alluding to his attitude afterwards to Marjorie, he called it "Pulling the old girl's leg." And when Marjorie had turned on him, her eyes had flashed scorn on him, her little body had quivered and shaken with indignation.

"If you think it clever currying favour with aunt by—by crawling to her," she cried, "then I don't! If you want to—to keep my respect, you'll have to act like a man, a man with self-respect! I—I hate to see you cringing to aunt, it makes me detest you. What does it matter if she has money? Do you want her money? Do you want her money more than you want me?"

"Goo-law, old girl, I—"

"Don't talk to me!" cried Marjorie. "Be a man, or I shall hate you!" And she had left him rubbing his chin thoughtfully, and wondering at the ways of women and of Marjorie Linden in particular.

"Blinking little spitfire, that's what she is!" he thought. "If she means to grow like the old girl, then—then—Hello, here's old Alston!"

Hugh could give Tom Arundel a matter of eight years, and therefore Tom regarded him as elderly. "A decent old bird!" was his favourite estimate.

"Hello!" said Hugh. "What's the matter? Not been rowing, have you? Tom, not rowing with the little girl, eh?"

Hugh's face was serious, for he had caught a glimpse of Marjorie a while ago hurrying through the garden, and the look on her face had sent him to find Tom.

"Not worrying—her or rowing her?"

"No, goodness knows I haven't said a word, but she flew at me and bit me!"

"Did what?"

"Metaphorically, of course," said Tom. "I say, Alston, do you think Marjorie is going to grow like her aunt?"

"Look here," said Hugh, and he gripped Tom by the shoulder with such strength that Tom was surprised and a little pained. "Look here, I don't know what Marjorie is going to grow like, but I know this—that she is the sweetest, most tender-hearted, dearest little soul, loyal and true and straight, and because you've won her love, my good lad, you ought to go down on your knees and thank Heaven for it. She's worth ten, fifty, a hundred of you and of me. A good woman—and Marjorie is that—a good woman, I tell you, is better, infinitely better, than the finest man that walks; and you are not that, not by a long way, Tom Arundel. So if you've offended the child, go after her. Ask her to forgive you and ask her humbly. You hear me? Ask her deucedly humbly, my lad! And listen to this—if you bring one tear to her eyes, one tear, one little stab to that tender heart of hers, if you—you bring one breath of sorrow and sadness into her life, I'll break your confounded neck for you! Have you got that, Tom Arundel?"

A final shake that made Tom's teeth rattle, and Hugh turned and strode away to find Marjorie. Tom Arundel stared after him.

"Well, I—hang me! Hang me if I don't believe old Alston's in love with her himself!"

Hugh Alston had meant to run over to Hurst Dormer and see how things were getting on there, and incidentally to collect any letters that might have come for him. But the days passed, and Hugh did not go. Lady Linden required her fat horses for her own purposes. Marjorie's own little ancient car had developed a serious internal complaint that had put it definitely out of commission, so there was no means of getting to Hurst Dormer unless he walked, or wired to his man to bring over his own car, but Hugh did not trouble to do that. They did not want him there, everything would be all right, so Joan's letter, with others, was propped up on the mantelpiece in his study and dusted carefully every morning; and Joan watched the post in vain, and with a growing sense of anger and humiliation in her breast.

But of this Hugh knew nothing. He was watching Marjorie and Tom. Somehow his sacrifice did not seem to have brought about the happy results that he had hoped for.

So Hugh, though he had little understanding of women, felt yet that things were not as they should be and as Marjorie of course could not possibly be to blame, it must be Tom Arundel, and to Tom he addressed himself forcibly.

Tom listened resentfully. "Look here, Alston, I don't know what the lay is," he said. "I don't know what's the matter. I am not conscious of having offended her. If I have, I am sorry—why goo-law, I worship the ground the little thing treads on!"

And Hugh, looking Tom straight in the eyes, knew that he was speaking the truth.

"Good!" he said. "I'm glad to hear it, and she's worth it!"

"And—and it hurts me, by George it does, Alston," Tom said, "the way she cuts up rough with me. And now you go for me bald-headed, as if I'd behaved like a pig to her. Why goo-law, man, I'd lie down and let her jump on me. I'd go and drown myself if it would cause her any—any amusement."

There was a distinct suggestion of tears in the boy's eyes, and Hugh turned hastily away.

"Marjorie dear," he was saying a while later, "what's wrong? Tell me all about it. Tell your old friend Hugh, and see if he can put things right."

"There is nothing—nothing wrong, Hugh!" Marjorie gasped. "Nothing! Nothing in the world!" And she belied her statement by suddenly sobbing and hiding her face against his shoulder.

"There, there—there!" he said, feeling as awkward as a man must feel when a woman cries to him. He patted her shoulder with the uncomfortable feeling that he was behaving like an idiot.

"It—it is nothing!" she gasped. "Hugh, it is really nothing!"

"Tom's a good lad, one of the best—clean through and through!"

"Yes, I know he is, and—and oh, I do know it, Hugh, and it isn't Tom's fault!"

"Your aunt's been worrying you?"

Henry St. John Cooper

"No, it is not that—oh, it is nothing, nothing in the world. It is only that I am a—a—little fool, an ungrateful, silly, little fool!"

And Hugh was frankly puzzled.

"You're going to be as happy as the day is long, little girl," he said. "Tom loves you, worships the ground you walk on; I think you're going to be the happiest girl alive. Dry your tears, dear, and smile as you used to in the old days!" He stooped over her and pressed a kiss on her shining hair; and there came to her a mad, passionate longing to lift her arms and clasp them about his neck and confess all, confess her stupidity and her blindness and her folly.

"It is you—you are the man I love. It is you I want—you all the time!" She longed to say it, but did not, and Hugh Alston never knew.

Hurst Dormer looked empty, and seemed silent and dull after Cornbridge. No place was dull and certainly no place was silent where Lady Linden was, and coming back to Hurst Dormer, Hugh felt as if he was then entering into a desert of solitude and silence.

"Everything has been quite all right," said Mrs. Morrisey. "The men have got on nicely with their work. Lane has taken advantage of your being away to give the car a thorough overhaul, and—and I think that is all, sir. There are a few letters waiting for you. I'll get them."

From whom this letter? Whose hand this? He wondered. He had never seen "Her" writing before, yet instinct told him that this was hers.

Two minutes later Hugh Alston was behaving like a lunatic.

"Mrs. Morrisey! Mrs. Morrisey! When did this letter come?"

"Oh, that one, sir? It came ten days ago—the very day you left, the same evening."

"Then why—why in the name of Heaven—" he began, and then stopped himself, for he remembered that he had ordered no letters should be sent on.

"I hope it is not important, sir?"

"Important!" he said. "Oh no, not at all, nothing important!" Again he read—

> "Because you have placed me in an intolerable position, and have subjected me to insult and annoyance, past all bearing, I ask you to meet me in London at the earliest opportunity..."

At the earliest opportunity! And those words had been written eleven days ago; and she had underscored the word "earliest" three times. Eleven days ago! "I feel I have a right to appeal to you for protection...."

She had written that, an appeal to him, and he had not until now read the written words.

What was she thinking of him? What could she think of his long silence?

He could not blame Mrs. Morrisey. There was only himself to blame, no one else! And there had he been, cooling his heels at Cornbridge and interfering with other folks' love affairs, and all the time Joan—Joan was perhaps wondering, watching, waiting for the answer that never came.

Henry St. John Cooper

He wanted to send a frantic telegram; but he did nothing of the kind. He wrote instead.

"I have been away. Only a few minutes ago did your letter reach me. I am at your service in all things. Heaven knows I bitterly regret the annoyance that you have been caused through me. You ask me to meet you in London. Do you not know that I will come most willingly, eagerly. I am writing this on the evening of Tuesday. You should receive my letter on Wednesday, probably in the evening; but in case it may be delayed, I suggest that you meet me in London on Thursday afternoon"—he paused, racking his brain for some suitable meeting place—"at four o'clock, in the Winter Garden of the Empire Hotel. Do not trouble to reply. I shall be there without fail, and shall then be, as I am now, and will ever be,

"Yours to command,
"HUGH ALSTON."

This letter he wrote hurriedly, and raced off with it to catch the post.

Seven, eight, ten days ago since Joan had written that letter, and there had come no reply. The man had ignored her, had treated her with silent contempt. The thought made her face burn, brought a sense of miserable self-abasement to her. She had pleaded to him for help, and he had treated her with silence and contempt.

Well, what did it matter? She hated him. She had always hated him. She laughed aloud and bitterly at her own thoughts. "Yes," she repeated to herself, "I hate him. I feel nothing but scorn and contempt for him. I am glad he did not answer my letter. I hope that I shall never see him again. If we do meet, by some mischance, then I shall pass him by."

Several times this morning Helen had looked curiously at Joan. For Helen was in a secret that as yet Joan did not share. It was a little conspiracy, with Helen as the prime mover in it.

"I am sure that there never was anything between Joan and that Hugh Alston. It was some foolish tittle-tattle, some nonsense, probably hatched by that stupid old talkative Lady Linden."

Two days ago had come a letter for Helen Everard, with an Australian stamp on it. It was from Jessie, her only sister, urging her to come out to her there, reminding her of an old promise to make a home in that distant land with her and her children. And Helen knew she must go. She wanted to go, had always meant to go, for Jessie's boys were very dear to her. Yet to leave Joan alone in this great house, so utterly alone!

Last night Helen had driven over quietly to Buddesby, and she and Constance had had a long talk.

"I can't leave Joan alone. I have written to Jessie, telling her that I shall start in three months. I have said nothing to Joan yet; but, Connie, I can't leave her alone!"

"Helen, do you think she could care for Johnny enough to become his wife?"

"I believe she is fond of him. I will not say that I think she is desperately in love, but she likes him and trusts him, as she must; and so, Connie, I hope it may come about. Joan will make an ideal wife. He is all a woman could wish and hope for, the truest, dearest, straightest man living, and so— Connie—I hope—"

"I will talk to him to-night, and I will suggest that he comes over to-morrow and puts his fate to the test. I know he loves her."

And to-day Johnny Everard should be here, if he had listened to his sister's advice, and that was a thing that Johnny ever did, save in the matter of hops.

There was a look of subdued eagerness, of visible nervousness and uncertainty, about Mr. John Everard that day. And Helen saw it.

"Joan's in the garden, John," she said.

"Yes, I—" He fumbled nervously with his hands.

"Helen, I have been talking to Con, at least Con's been talking to me!"

"Yes, dear?"

"And she—she says—Con tells me that there is a chance for me—just a chance, Helen. And, Helen, I don't want to spoil my chance, if I have one, by rushing in. You understand?"

"I think," Helen said, "that Joan would like you the better and admire you the more for being brave enough to speak out."

"That's it! I've got to speak out. You know I love her!"

"I do, dear."

"But she doesn't love me. It is not likely; how could she? Look at me, a great ugly chap—how could such a girl care for me?"

"I think any girl might very easily care for you, Johnny!"

"An ugly brute like me? A farmer. I am nothing more, Helen, and—and—"

"Johnny, she is in the garden. Go to her; take your courage in both your hands. Remember—

'He either fears his fate too much.
Or his deserts are small,
That dares not put it to the touch,
To gain or lose it all.'"

"I'll go!" Johnny Everard said. "I can but lose, eh? That's the worst that can happen to me—lose. But, by Heaven! if I do lose, it is going to—to hurt, and hurt badly. Helen dear, wish me luck!"

She put both her hands on his broad shoulders and kissed him on the forehead. She felt to him as a mother might.

"From my heart, Johnny, I wish you luck and fortune and happiness," she said.

Joan was at the far end of the wide, far-spreading garden. She was seated on a bench beside a pool where grew water-lilies, and where in the summer sunshine the dragon-flies skimmed on the placid surface of the green water—water that now and again was broken into a ripple by the quick twist of the tail of one of the fat old carp that lived their humdrum, adventureless years in the quiet depths.

She sat here, chin in hand, grey eyes watching the pool, yet seeing nothing of its beauties, and her thoughts away, away with a man who had insulted her, had brought trouble and shame and anger to her—a man to whom she had appealed, and had appealed in vain; a man dead to all manhood, a man she hated—yes, hated—for often she told herself so, and it must be true.

And then suddenly she heard the fall of a footstep on the soft turf behind her, and, turning, looked into the face of a man whose eyes were filled with love for her.

So for one long moment they looked at one another, and the colour rose in the girl's cheeks, and into her eyes there came a wistful regret. For she knew why this man was here. She knew what he had to say to her, to ask of her, here by the green pool.

## CHAPTER XXIV

## "—TO GAIN, OR LOSE IT ALL"

"Take your courage in both hands" Helen had said to him, and he was doing so; but Johnny Everard knew himself for a coward at this moment.

He felt tongue-tied, more than usually awkward, terribly and shamefully nervous. Yet the grey eyes were on his face, and he knew that he must speak, must put all to the hazard. And he knew also that if to-day he lost her, it would be the biggest and the blackest sorrow of his life, something that he would never live down, never forget.

Oh, it was worth fighting for, worth taking his courage in both hands for, this girl with the sweet, serious face and the tender mouth, the great, enquiring, yet trusting grey eyes. He had seen her cold, stately, a little unapproachable, but he had never seen scorn in those eyes. He had never seen the red lips curled with contempt. He knew nothing of her in this guise, as another man did.

And now the girl seemed to be all woman, tender, sympathetic, and the courage came to him; he sate himself beside her and took her hand in his, and it gave him hope that she did not draw it away.

Henry St. John Cooper

What he said, how he said it, how he stumbled over his story of love and devotion he never knew. But it was an honest story, a story that did him honour, and did honour too to the woman he told it to.

"I love you, dear. I have loved you from the moment I first saw you. I know you are high above me. I know what I am, an unlovely sort of fellow, rough and—and not fit to touch your hand—" for, being deeply in love, his opinion of himself had naturally sunk to zero. The perfection of the beloved object always makes an honest man painfully conscious of his own inferiority and unworthiness. And so it was with Johnny Everard, this day beside the green pool. And the slim, cool hand was not withdrawn.

"Johnny, what are you asking me? Why have you come here to me? What do you want—of me?" she asked, yet did not look him in the face, but sat with eyes resting on the placid water.

"Just to tell you that—to tell you how I love you, Joan."

Another man had told her that; the echo of his words came back to her from the past. How often those words of his had come back; she could never forget them. Yet she told herself that she hated him who had uttered them, hated him, for was he not a proved craven?

*("If, in telling you that I love you, is a sin fast all forgiveness, I glory in it. I take not one word of it back.")*

And now another, a worthier, better man, was telling her the same story, holding her hand, and, she knew, looking into her face; yet her eyes did not meet his.

And, listening to him, her heart grew more bitter than ever

before to the man who had uttered those words she would never forget, bitter against him, yet more against herself. For she was conscious of shame and anger—at her woman's weakness, at the folly of which her woman's heart was capable.

"I know I am not fit for you, not good enough for you, Joan. There isn't a man living who would be—but—I love you—dear, and with God's help I would try to make you a happy woman."

Manly words, honest and sincere, she knew, as must be all that this man said and did—a man to rely on, a very tower of strength; a man to protect her, a man to whom she could take her troubles and her secrets, knowing full well that he would not fail her.

And while these thoughts passed in her mind she sat there silently, her hand in his, and never thought to draw it away.

"Joan, will you be my wife, dear? I am asking for more than I could ever deserve. There is nothing about me that makes me worthy of that great happiness and honour, save one thing—my love for you."

"And yet," she said, and broke her silence for the first time, "there is one question that you do not ask me, Johnny."

"One question?"

"You do not ask me if I love you!"

"How can I ask for the impossible, the unlikely? There is nothing in me for such a girl as you to love."

"There is much in you for any woman to love. There is

honesty and truth and bravery, and a clean sweet mind. I know all that, I know that you are a good man, Johnny. I know that; but oh, I do not love you!"

"I know," he said sadly. "I know that." And his hand seemed to slip away from hers.

"And you would not—not take me—Johnny, without love?" she asked, and her voice trembled.

"Joan, I—I don't understand. I am a foolish, dense fellow, dear, and I don't understand!"

She turned to him, and now her eyes met his frankly, and never had he seen them so soft, so tender, so filled with a strange and wonderful light, the light that is born of tenderness and sympathy and kindliness.

"Would you make me your wife, Johnny, knowing that I—I do not love you as a woman should love the man she takes for her husband."

"I—I would try to teach you, dear. I would try to win a little of your heart."

"And that would content you, Johnny?"

"It must. I dare not ask too much, and I—I—love you so!"

*("I glory in it. I take not one word of it lack!")*

Hateful words, words she could never forget, that came back to torture and fill her with a sense of shame. Strange that they were dinning in her memory, even now.

*("I glory in it. I take not one word back!")*

And then suddenly she made a gesture, as to fling off remembrance. She turned more fully to him, and her eyes met his frankly.

"I do not love you, dear, as a woman should love the man she mates with; but I like you. I honour you and trust you, and if—if you will take me as I am, not asking for too much, not asking, dear, for more than I can give—"

"Joan," he said, "my Joan!"

She bent her head.

"If you will take me—as I am, not asking for more than I can give, then—then I will come to you, if you will have it so. But oh, my dear, you are worth more than this, far more than this!"

He lifted her hand and held it to his lips, the only embrace that in his humility he dare offer her. And even while she felt his lips upon her hand, there came back to her memory eyes that glowed with love and passion, a deep voice that shook with feeling—

*("I glory in it, and take not one word of it back!")*

# CHAPTER XXV

## IN THE MIRE

Women, chattering over their tea in the lounge of the Empire Hotel, followed the tall restless young man with their eyes. He was worth looking at, so big and fine, and bronzed, and so worried, so anxious-looking, poor fellow.

Four o'clock, a quarter past, half past. She would not come. Of course she would not come; he had offended past all forgiveness in taking so long to reply to her appeal. Hugh Alston cursed the unlucky star that he must have been born under.

Two middle-aged women, seated at a small table, taking their tea after strenuous shopping at the sales, watched him and discussed him frankly.

"Evidently here to meet someone!"

"And she hasn't come!"

"You can see how disappointed he looks, poor fellow."

"Too bad of her!"

"My dear, what some men can see in some women..."

"And a girl who would keep a man like that waiting deserves to lose him."

"I hope she does. See, he's going now. I hope she comes later and is disappointed."

"Oh no, I think that must be she. What a handsome girl, but how cold and proud looking!"

She had come, even as he was giving up in despair. As he turned to leave, she came, and they met face to face.

The two amiable busybodies sipped their tea and watched.

"My dear, she didn't even offer him her hand—such a cold and stately bow. They can't be lovers, after all!"

"I don't think I ever saw a more lovely girl!"

"But icily cold. That pink chiffon I bought at Robinson's will make up into a charming evening dress for Irene, don't you think?"

"I am afraid I am late," Joan said, and her voice was clear and cold, expressionless as a voice could be.

"Surely I deserve that at least, after the unforgivable delay in answering your letter."

"Yes," she said, "you—you were a long time answering." And suddenly she realised what that delay had meant.

Yesterday, if his answer had come, perhaps she would not have done as she had done. But it was done now, past recall.

"I was away. I found Hurst Dormer irksome and lonely. Lady Linden came over; she invited me to stay at Cornbridge," he explained. "So I went, and no letters were forwarded. Yours came within a few hours of my leaving. I hope you understand that if I had had it—"

"You would have answered it before, Mr. Alston? Yes, I am glad to feel the neglect was not intentional."

"Intentional!"

"I—I thought, judging from the manner in which we last parted, and what you then said to me, that you—you preferred not to—see me again."

"I was hurt then, hurt and bitter. I had no right to say what I said. I ask you to accept my apologies, Joan."

She started a little at the sound of her name, but did not look at him.

"Perhaps you were right. I have thought it over since. Yes, I think I acted meanly; it was a thing a woman would do. That is where a woman fails—in small things—ideas, mean ideas come to her mind, just like that one. A man would not think such things. Yes, I am ashamed by the smallness of it. You said 'ungenerous.' I think a better expression would have been 'mean-spirited.'"

"Joan!"

"But we need not discuss that. We owe one another apologies. Shall we take it that they are offered and accepted?"

He nodded. "Tea?" he asked, "or coffee?" For the hotel servant had come for his orders.

"Tea, please," she said; "and—and this time I will not ask for the bill." The faintest flicker of a smile crossed her lips, and then was gone, and he thought that in its place a look of weariness and unhappiness came into the girl's face.

She had sent for him to ask his help. His letter had only reached her that morning, and when she had read it, she had asked herself, "Shall I go? Shall I see him?" And had answered "No! It is over; I do not need his help now. I have someone else to whom I must turn for help, someone who will give it readily."

And yet she had come—that is the way of women. And because she had come, she would still ask his help, and not ask it of that other. For surely he who had brought all this trouble on to her should be the one to clear her path?

The waiter brought the tea, and Hugh leaned back and watched her as she poured it out. And, watching her, there came to him a vision of the bright morning room at Hurst Dormer, a vision of all the old familiar things he had known since boyhood: and in that vision, that day-dream, he saw her sitting where his mother once had sat, and she was pouring out tea, even as now.

A clearer, stronger vision this than any he had had in the old days of Marjorie. He smiled at the thought of those dreams, so utterly broken and dead and wafted away into the nothingness of which they had been built.

"You sent for me to help you?"

"Yes!" A tinge of colour rose in her cheeks and waxed till her cheeks and even her throat were flooded with a brilliant, glorious flush, and then, suddenly as it had come, it died away again, leaving her whiter than before.

Henry St. John Cooper

"I wanted your help. I felt that I had a right to ask it, seeing that you—you—"

"Have caused you trouble and annoyance? You wrote that," he said.

She bowed her head.

"What you did, has brought more trouble, more shame, more annoyance to me than I can ever explain. I do not ask you to tell me why you did it—it was cruel and mean, unmanly; but you did it. And it can never be undone, so I ask for no reasons, no explanations. They—they do not interest me now. You have brought me trouble and—even danger—and so I turned to you, to ask your help. I have the right, have I not the right—to demand it?"

"The greatest right on earth," he said. "Joan, how can I help you?"

But she did not answer immediately, for the answer would be difficult.

"When you played with a woman's name," she said, "you played with the most fragile, the most delicate and easily breakable thing there is. Do you realise that? A woman's fair name is her most sacred possession, and yet you played with mine, used it for your own purpose, and so have brought me to shame and misery."

"Joan," he leaned towards her, "how—how—tell me how?"

"Three days ago," she said quietly, "I submitted and paid three thousand pounds blackmail, rather than that your name and mine, linked together, should be dragged in the mire!"

It was almost as though those white hands of hers had struck him a heavy blow between the eyes. Hugh sat and stared at her in amaze.

Her words seemed obscure, scarcely possible to understand, yet he had gathered in the sense of them.

"Three days ago I submitted and paid three thousand pounds blackmail rather than your name and mine, linked together, should be dragged in the mire."

A girl might well shrink to tell a man what she must tell him, to go into explanations that were an offence to the purity of her mind. Yet, listening to her, looking at her, at the pale, proud young face, white as marble, Hugh Alston knew that he had never admired and reverenced her as he did now.

"The story that you told of our marriage, that lie that I can never understand, passed from lip to lip. Many have heard it; it has caused many to wonder. I do not ask why you uttered it. It does not matter now, nothing matters, save that you did utter it, and it has gone abroad. Then one day you came to the office where I was employed, and the man who employed me put his private room at your disposal, knowing that by means of some spyhole he had contrived he could hear all that passed between us. And then you offered me marriage—by way of atonement. Do you remember? You offered to—to atone by marrying me."

"In my mad, presumptuous folly, Joan!"

"And it was overheard; the man heard all. He did not understand—how should he? His vile mind grasped at other meanings. He went down to Marlbury and to Morchester to make enquiries, to look for an entry in a register that was never made. He went to General Bartholomew and then

Cornbridge, where he saw Lady Linden, and heard from her all that she had to tell, and then—then he came to me. He told me that he knew the truth, and that if I would marry him he would forgive—forgive everything!"

Hugh Alston said nothing. He sat with his big hands gripped hard, and thinking of Philip Slotman a red fury passed like a mist before his eyes.

"I told him to go, and then came a letter from him, a friendly letter, a letter that could not cause him any trouble. He assured me of his friendship and of his—silence, you understand, his silence—and asked me as a friend to lend him three thousand pounds. It was blackmail—oh, I knew that. I hesitated, and did not know what to do. There was none to whom I could turn—no one. I had no friend. Helen Everard is only a friend of a few short weeks. I felt that I could not go to her, I felt somehow that she would never understand. And then—then at last, because, I suppose, I am a woman and therefore a coward, and because I was so alone—so helpless—I sent the money."

"Oh, that I—"

"Remember," she said, "remember I had written to you, asking your help. I had waited days, and no answer had come. I had no right to believe that I could ask your help."

"Joan, Joan, didn't you know that you could? Have you forgotten what I told you once—that stands true to-day as then, will stand true to the last hour of my life. I have brought shame and misery on you, God forgive me—yet unintentionally, Joan." He leaned forward, and grasped at her hand and held it, though she would have drawn it free of him. "I told you that I loved you that night. I love you now—my love for you gives me the right to protect you!"

"You have no rights, no rights," she said, and drew her hand away.

"Because you will not give me those rights. I asked you to marry me once. I came to you, thinking in my small soul that I was doing a fine thing, offering atonement—my—my very words, atonement—for the evil I had unwittingly done. And you refused to accept the prize!" He laughed bitterly. "You refused with scorn, just scorn, Joan. You made me realise that I had but added to my offence. I—I to offer you marriage, in my lordly way, when I should have sued on my knees to you for forgiveness, as I would sue now, humbly and contritely, offering love and love alone—love and worship and service to the end of my days, as please Heaven I shall sue, Joan."

"You cannot!" she said quietly. "You cannot, and if you should, the answer will be the same, as then!"

"Because you can never forgive?"

"Because I have no power to give what you would ask for!"

"Your love?"

She did not answer. She turned her face away, for she knew she could not in truth say "No" to that, for the knowledge that she had been trying to stifle was with her now, the knowledge that meant that she could not love the man whose wife she had promised to be.

"My—my hand—" she said.

And he, not understanding for the moment, looked at her, and then suddenly understanding came to him.

"You—you mean?"

"You—you did not answer my letter, and I—I waited," she said, and her voice was low and muffled. There was no pride in her face now; all its hardness, all its bitterness and scorn were gone.

"I waited and waited—and thought—hoped," she said, "and nothing came. And yesterday a man—a man I like and admire, a fine man, a good man, honest and noble, a man who—who loves me better than I deserve, came to me—and—and so to-day it is too late! Though," she cried, with a touch of scorn for herself, "it would have made no difference—nothing would have made any difference. You—you understand that I scarcely know what I am saying!"

"You have given your promise to another man?" he asked quietly.

"Yes!"

"And you do not love him?"

"He's a man," she cried, "a man who would not make a jest of a woman's name."

"And even so, you do not love him, because that would not be possible."

"You have no right to say that," and she wrenched her hand free.

"I have the right, the right you gave me."

"I—I gave you no right."

"You have. You gave me that right, Joan, when you gave me your heart. You do not love that man, because you love me!"

Back into the white face came all the hardness and coldness that he so well knew. She rose; she looked down on him.

"It is—untrue. I do not. I have but one feeling for you always—always—the same, the one feeling. I despise you. How could I love a thing that I despise?"

And, knowing that it was a lie, she dared not meet the scrutiny of his eyes, and turned quickly away.

"Joan!" he said. He would have followed her, but then came the waiter with his bill, and he was forced to stay, and when he reached the street she was gone.

"I quite thought that they were going to make it up, and then it seemed that they quarrelled again," one of the ladies at the other table said.

The other nodded. "I think that they do not know their own minds, young people seldom do. I wish I had bought three yards more of that cerise ninon. It would have made up so well for Violet, don't you think?"

# CHAPTER XXVI

## MR. ALSTON CALLS

Mr. Philip Slotman sat in his office; he was slowly deciphering a letter, ill-written and badly spelled.

"DEAR SIR,

"According to promise I am writing to you hopeing it finds you as it leaves me at present. Dear sir, having some news I am writing to tell you saime. Yesterday Mr. John Everard of Buddesby was here and him and Miss Jone was in the garden for a long time. I seen them from my window, but could not get near enuff to hear. Anyhow I see him kissing her hand. Laiter, after he had gone, I seen Miss Jone and Mrs. Everard together, and listened as best I could. From what I heard I imadgined that Miss Jone and Mr. John Everard is now engaged to be married, which Mrs. Everard seems very pleased to hear.

"This morning Miss Jone gets a letter and the postmark is Hurst Dormer, like you told me to look out for. She is now gone to London. Please send money in accordance with promise and I will write and tell you all the news as soon as there is any more.

"Youres truley,

"MISS ALICE BETTS."

The door opened, a boy clerk came in. Slotman thrust the letter he had been reading into an open drawer.

"What is it? What do you want?"

"A gentleman to see you, sir. Mr. Alston from—"

"I can't see him!" Slotman said quickly. "Tell him I am out, and that—"

"I am already here, and you are going to see me." Hugh Alston came in. "You can go!" to the boy, who hesitated. "You hear me, you can go!"

Hugh closed the door after the lad.

"You're not going to be too busy to see me this morning, Slotman, for I have interesting things to discuss with you."

"I am a busy man," Slotman began nervously.

"Very!" said Hugh—"very, so I hear."

He stepped into the room, and faced Slotman across the paper-littered table.

"I have been hearing about some of your enterprises," he said, and there was that in his face that caused Mr. Slotman a feeling of insecurity and uneasiness. "One of them is blackmail!"

"How dare—" Slotman began, with an attempt at bluster.

"That's what I am here for; to dare. You have been black-mailing a young lady whose name we need not mention. You have obtained the sum of three thousand pounds from her, by means of threats. I want that money—and more; I want a declaration from you that you will never molest her again; for if you do—if you do—"

Hugh's face was not good to see, and Mr. Slotman quivered uneasily in his chair.

"The—the money was lent to me. Miss Meredyth worked for me, and—and I went to her, explaining that my business was in a precarious condition, and she very kindly lent me the money. And I haven't got it, Mr. Alston. I'll swear I haven't a penny of it left. I could not repay it if I wanted to; it—it was a friendly loan."

Slotman leaned back in his chair; he looked at Hugh.

"You have done me a cruel wrong, Mr. Alston," he said, in the tone of a deeply injured man. "Miss Meredyth worked for me, and while she was here I respected her, even more." He paused. "At any rate I respected her. She attracted me, and, I will confess it, I fell in love with her. She was poor; she had nothing then to tempt a fortune hunter, and thank Heaven I can say I was never that. I asked her to be my wife, no man could do more, no man could act more honourably. You'll admit that, eh? You must admit that?"

"And she refused you?"

"Not—not definitely. It was too good an offer for a girl in her position to refuse without consideration."

"You lie!"

Slotman shifted uneasily. "I cannot force your belief."

"You're right, you can't. Well, go on—what more?"

"She came into this money; my proposal no longer tempted her. She then refused me, even though I told her that the past—her past—would be forgotten, that I would never refer to it."

"What past?" Hugh shouted.

"Hers and yours," Slotman said boldly. "A supposed marriage that never took place, her sudden disappearance from her school in June, nineteen hundred and eighteen, when that marriage was supposed to have been celebrated— but never was. Her story of leaving England for Australia— an obvious lie, Mr. Alston. All those things I knew. All those things I can prove—against her—and against you—and— and—" Slotman's voice quivered. He leaped to his feet and uttered a shout for help.

The blood-red mist was before Hugh's eyes, and out of that mist appeared a vision of a face, an unpleasant face, with starting eyes and gaping mouth.

This he saw, and then his vision cleared, and with a shudder he released his hold on the man's throat, and Philip Slotman subsided limply into his chair.

Henry St. John Cooper

# CHAPTER XXVII

## THE WATCHER

Helen Everard's pleasant face was beaming. Her smile expressed complete contentment and satisfaction, for everything was going as everything should go. Johnny was an accepted lover, Joan's future would be protected; she herself would be left free to make her long journey to the dear ones at the other side of the world. All was well!

Joan had been to London yesterday, had rushed off with scarcely a word, and had returned at night, tired and seemingly dispirited.

Joan, quiet and calm, smiled at Helen and kissed her good morning, but spoke hardly at all.

"You had a tiring day in Town yesterday, dear?"

"Very!"

"Shopping?"

"No!"

Helen asked no more questions. She thought of Hugh Alston.

Could it be anything to do with him? She could never quite understand the position of Hugh Alston. Of course the talk about a marriage having taken place years ago between Hugh Alston and Joan was absurd, was ridiculous. Joan was proving the absurdity of it even now by accepting Johnny.

"Connie is coming over this afternoon to see you, Joan," she said. "She sent me a note over yesterday by a boy. Johnny has told her of course, and Connie is delighted beyond words. She sends you her dear love."

"Thank you!" Joan said calmly.

"Of course," Helen hesitated, "the marriage need not be long delayed. You see—" She paused, and then went into explanations about Jessie and the children out in Australia, and her own promise to go to them.

"So this afternoon I want you and Connie to have a long, long talk," Helen said. "There will be so much for you to discuss. Connie is the business man, you know. Poor Johnny is hopeless when it comes to discussing things and—and arrangements. Of course, dear, you quite understand that Johnny is not well off."

"I know, but that does not matter."

"I know, but even though Johnny is one of the finest and straightest men living, it will be better if in some way your own money is so tied up that it belongs to you and to you only. Johnny himself would wish it. He doesn't want to touch one penny of your money!"

"I am sure of that." Joan rose. She went out into the garden. She wanted to get away from Helen's well-meant, friendly, affectionate chatter about the future, and about money and marriage. She went to the bench beside the pool and sat there, staring at the green water.

"It was true," she whispered to herself, "all true, what I said. I—I do despise him. How could I love a thing that I despised; and I do despise him!"

It was not of Johnny Everard she was thinking.

"He said—he said that he had a right, that my love for him gave him the right! How dared he?" A deep flush stole into her cheeks, and then died out.

She rose suddenly with a gesture of impatience.

"It is a lie! It is wrong, and it is nonsense. I am engaged to marry Johnny Everard, and there is no finer, better man living! I shall never see that other man again. Yesterday he and I parted for good and for always, and I am glad—glad!" And she knew even while she uttered the words that she was very miserable.

Connie Everard drove the pony-trap over to Starden. She brought with her a boy who would drive it back again. Later in the afternoon Johnny would drive the car over for her and take her back.

Connie, having attended carefully to her toilet, descended to the waiting pony-trap, and found, to her surprise and a little to her annoyance, that Ellice was already seated in the little vehicle.

"Ellice, dear, I am sorry, but—"

"You don't want to take me, Connie; but, all the same, I am going. I want to see—her!"

"Why?"

"I want to see her," the girl said. A dusky glow of sudden passion came into her face. "I want to see her. There is no harm, is there?" She laughed shrilly. "I shan't hurt her by looking at her. I want to see her again, the woman that he loves." There was a shake in her voice, a suggestion of passionate tears, but the child held herself in check.

"Ellice, darling, it will be better if you—"

"If I don't go. I know, but I am going. You—you can't turn me out, Connie. I am too strong; I shall cling to the sides of the cart."

There was a look, half of laughter, half of defiance, in the girl's eyes.

"Connie, I am going, and nothing shall prevent me!"

Connie sighed, and stepped into the cart and took up the reins. "Very well, dear!" she said resignedly.

"You are angry with me, Connie?"

"Why should you want to go to Starden?"

"I want to see her again. I want to—to understand, to—to know things."

"What do you mean, to understand, to know things?"

"I want to watch her!"

"Ellice, you will make me angry presently. Ellice," Connie added suddenly, "I suppose you don't intend to make a scene, and make yourself foolish and—and cheap?"

"I shall say nothing. I only want to watch and to try and understand."

"I think you are acting foolishly and wrongly, Ellice. I think you are a very foolish child!"

"I wish," Ellice said, and said it without passion, but with a deep certainty in her voice, "I wish that I were dead, Connie."

"You ought to be thoroughly ashamed of yourself," said Connie, who could think of nothing better to say.

She made one more attempt when Starden was reached.

"Ellice, child, why not go back with Hobbins?"

"I am coming with you," Ellice said.

"You—you will not—I mean you will—not be silly or rude to—"

Ellice drew herself up with a childish dignity. "I shall not forget that I am a lady, Connie," she said, and said it with such stateliness and such dignity that Connie felt no inclination to laugh.

Helen frowned. She was annoyed at the sight of Ellice, frankly she did not like the girl. Helen was a good, honest woman who liked everything that was good and honest. Ellice Brand might be good and honest, but there was something about the girl that was beyond Helen's ken. She was so elfin, so gipsy-like, so different from most girls Helen knew, and had known.

During the long afternoon, when they sat for a time in the garden, or in the shady drawing-room, Joan was aware of the fixed and intent gaze of a pair of dark eyes. Strangely and wonderfully dark were those eyes, and they seemed to possess some magnetic power, a power of making themselves felt. More than once in the middle of saying something to Helen or to Connie, Joan found herself at a loss for words, and impelled by some unknown force to turn her head and look straight into those eyes that blazed in the little white face.

Why did the girl stare at her so? Why, Joan wondered? A strange, elfin-like child, a bud on the point of bursting into a wondrous beauty, Joan realised, and realised too that there was enmity in the dark eyes that stared at her so mercilessly.

"Ellice, child, go out into the garden," Helen said presently. "Come with me, we will leave Connie and Joan to have a little talk. Come, there are lots of things to see. This is a wonderful garden, you know—far, far better than Buddesby."

"It isn't," Ellice said quietly. "There's no garden in the world like Buddesby garden, and no place in the world like Buddesby, but I will come with you if you want me to."

"A strange girl!" Joan said.

"A very dear, good, lovable, but passionate child," Connie said. "Now let us talk of you and Johnny, Joan, of the future. Helen has told you that—that she—"

"She wishes to leave us soon? Yes."

"And so," Connie slipped her hand into Joan's, "the marriage need not be long delayed."

"Whenever—he wishes it," Joan said, and for her life she could not put any warmth into her voice, and Connie, who noticed most things, noticed the chill coldness of it.

"And yet she must love Johnny, or she would not marry him," Connie thought.

"I leave everything to you, and to Helen and to him."

It seemed almost as if Joan had a strange disinclination to utter Johnny's name. Johnny sounded so babyish, so childlike, so affectionate, yet she felt that she could not speak of him as "John." It would sound hard and crude in the ears of those who loved him, and called him by the more tender name.

It was another shock to Connie later when Johnny came. She watched for the greeting between these two, and felt shocked and startled when Johnny took Joan's hand and held it for a moment, then lifted it to his lips. No other kiss passed between them.

And Connie felt her own cheeks burning, and wondered why.

How strange! Lovers, and particularly accepted lovers, always kissed!

There was that about Johnny that for the first time in her life almost irritated Connie. She watched him, and saw that his eyes were following Joan with that look of strange, dog-like devotion that Connie remembered with a start she had herself surprised in Ellice's eyes before now.

And as she watched, so watched another, herself almost forgotten as she sat in a corner of the room. The big black eyes were on these two, drifting from the face of one to the face of the other, taking no heed, and no count of anything else but of these two affianced lovers.

Very clearly and almost coldly Joan had expressed her own wishes.

"If you wish the marriage to take place soon, I am content. I would like it to—to be—not very soon—not just yet," she added, and seemed to be speaking against her own will, and as though in opposition to her own thoughts. "Still, whatever you arrange, I will willingly agree to. I prefer to leave it all to you, Helen, and you, Connie, and—and you, Johnny. But it might take place just before Helen goes away. That would be time enough, would it not?"

"It was the very thing I was going to suggest," Helen said. "In three months' time then, Joan."

Joan bowed her head. "In three months' time then," she said.

They were all three very silent as Johnny drove the little car back to Buddesby that evening. The sun was down, but the twilight lingered. Ellice sat crushed in between Johnny's big bulk and Connie, and she would not have changed places with the queen on her throne.

"There's Rundle with that horrible lurcher dog of his," said Johnny, and spoke more to make conversation than anything else.

They could see the man, the village poacher, slouching along under a hedge with the ever-faithful dog close at heel.

"A horrible, fierce-looking beast," said Connie. "It fights with every dog in the place, and—"

"But it loves him; it loves its master," Ellice said passionately. "It would die for its master, wouldn't it?"

"Why, I daresay it would, Gipsy," Johnny said. "But why so excited about it, little girl?"

"If you—if you," Ellice said, "had the offer of two dogs, the one splendid, a thoroughbred deerhound, graceful, beautiful, fine to look at, but cold and with no love to give its master, and the other—a hideous beast like Rundle's lurcher—but a beast who could love and die for its master, and dying lick the hand of the master it loved, glad and grateful to—to die for him—which would you have, which would you have, Johnny?"

Johnny was hardly listening. He was looking down the dusky road and seeing in imagination a face, the most beautiful, wonderful face that his world had ever held.

"I don't know, Gipsy girl," he said. "I don't know!"

"No!" Ellice said; and her voice shook and quavered in an unnatural laugh. "You don't know, Johnny; you don't know!"

And Connie, who heard and understood, shivered a little at the sound of the girl's laughter.

# CHAPTER XXVIII

## "HE DOES NOT LOVE ME NOW"

"Tom," said Lady Linden, "is by no means a fool, Marjorie."

"No, aunt."

"He has ideas. I don't say that they are brilliant, but he gets the germ of a plan into his brain. And now I will tell you what he suggests about Partridge's cottage and land when the lease falls in."

Lady Linden proceeded to explain Tom Arundel's idea, and Marjorie sat and stared out into the garden and thought of Hugh.

Was he at Hurst Dormer now? If not, where was he? What was he doing? What was he thinking about? Did he still love her, or had he fallen in love with Joan? And, if he had, would he marry Joan? and if not.

"So there you see, and what do you think of that?" asked Lady Linden, coming to the end of her remarks.

"I think it would be very nice!"

Henry St. John Cooper

"Very nice!" Lady Linden snorted. "Very nice! What a feeble remark. My good Marjorie, do you take no intelligent interest in anything? Upon my word, now I come to look back I wonder at myself, I do indeed. I wonder at myself to think that a man like Hugh Alston, an intellectual, deep-thinking man, a man with common-sense and plenty of it—what was I saying? Oh yes, I wonder at myself for ever hoping or believing that a man like Hugh could fall in love with a silly little donkey like you. And yet men do, even clever men—I've known several quite clever men fall in love with perfect fools of women. But I was wrong, and you are right. I see it now. Tom Arundel is the man for you; you are fitted for one another. He is not quite a fool, but you are. He's not clever enough to be annoyed by your folly. Hugh, on the other hand, would positively dislike you after a month. There! don't howl, for goodness' sake—don't snivel, child! Run away and play with your doll"

"Patience!" said Lady Linden, when her niece went out—"I have the patience of ten Jobs rolled into one. She's a good little soul, but an awful idiot! And bless my wig!" added her ladyship, who did not wear one, but her own luxuriant hair, "what's that hopeless idiot of a Perkins doing with those standard roses?" She sallied out, battle in her eyes, to tell Perkins, the under-gardener, something about the culture of roses, and incidentally to point out what her opinion of himself was in plain and straightforward language.

Meanwhile, Marjorie had hurried out. It was not true! She was not so stupid and so silly that Hugh could never have fallen in love with her. Why, he had fallen in love with her! He had wanted her for his wife, and she—she in her blindness and her folly, in her stupidity, which her aunt had but now been flinging in her teeth, had not realised that he was the one man in her world, the only man, and that she loved him as never, never could she love Tom Arundel or anyone else.

The little ancient disreputable car had been repaired by Rodding, the village handyman, who by some conjuring trick had made it run again. Marjorie started it.

She had made up her mind. She would go to Hurst Dormer, she would see Hugh and—and quite what she would do she did not know. Everything was on the knees of the gods, only she knew that she was very unhappy, a very miserable, unhappy, foolish girl, who had got what she had asked for, and found that she did not want it now she had it.

Piff, piff, paff, paff went the car, and Marjorie rolled off with a succession of jerks, leaving behind an odoriferous cloud of smoke and exhaust gases that lay like a blue mist along the drive, and presently made Lady Linden cough and speak in uncomplimentary terms of motoring and motorists generally.

On to Hurst Dormer Marjorie plugged, sad at heart, realising her folly.

"It is my fault," she felt miserably; "it is all my fault, and I am not fair to Tom. He doesn't understand me. I see him look at me sometimes, and I don't wonder at it. He doesn't understand me a bit; he has every right to—to think—I love him, and I don't—I don't. I love Hugh!"

It was an hour later that Marjorie put in an appearance at Hurst Dormer.

Hugh was there, and Hugh was in. It brought relief. She wanted to cry with the relief she felt.

Over the tea-table, where she poured out the tea from the old silver Anne teapot, she looked at him, and saw many changes that one not loving him, as she knew she did now, might have missed. The cheery frank smile was there yet, but it had lost much of its happiness. His eyes were no less kind, but they had a tired look about them, a wistful look. Oh, that she might cheat herself into believing that their wistfulness was for her! But Marjorie was not the little fool her aunt called her. She was a woman, and was gifted with a woman's understanding.

"He does not love me now, not as he did. I had my chance, and I said no, and now—now it is gone for ever."

And he, leaning back in his chair, watched her pouring out the tea as he had a few days ago watched another pouring out tea in a London hotel. The sight of Joan performing that domestic duty had brought to him then a vision of this same old room, this very old teapot, that his mother had used. And now, seeing Marjorie here, pouring out the tea, the only vision, the only remembrance that it brought to him was the memory of another girl pouring out tea in a London hotel.

"Hugh, have you seen her—Joan?"

He started—started at the sound of the name that was forever in his thoughts.

"Yes, dear," he said simply, for why should he lie to this child?

"Oh!" she said. "Oh, and—and Hugh, she and you—" She paused, she held her face down that he might not see it.

"Joan Meredyth," he said slowly, "and I met in Town a few days ago. She told me then, that she is engaged to be married."

"Oh!" Marjorie said, and her heart leaped with a new-born hope.

"And I," Hugh went on, "am worried and anxious about her."

"Hugh!"

"I can't worry you, little girl. It is nothing in which you could help; it is my fault, my folly!"

"Mine!" she said.

"No, it is mine. The whole idea was mine; I shoulder the blame of it all. It has succeeded in what we attempted. You are all right, you and Tom. I've made a lovely mess of everything else. But that does not matter so much. What we wanted, we won, eh?" He smiled at her, little dreaming that she had only won dead-sea fruit.

"Why are you worried and anxious about Joan?"

"I am not going to tell you, dear. I can't very well. Besides, you couldn't help. You are happy, you are all right. Tom is in high favour with her ladyship, so that's good, and you—you and Tom are happy, eh?"

"Yes," she said miserably.

"He's a good fellow, Marjorie. Make allowances for him. He'll need 'em, he's no angel; but he means well, and he's a good clean, honest man, is Tom Arundel, and you'll be a happy girl when you are his wife; please God!" he added, and put his hand on her shoulder, and did not notice that she was weeping silently.

He drove her back to Cornbridge in the moonlight, and left

Henry St. John Cooper

her at the gates of the Manor House. "Little girl," he said, "in this life there's a good deal of give and take. Don't expect too much, and don't be hurt if you don't get everything that you ask for. Remember this—I—I cared for you very much." "Cared!" she thought. "Cared?" He spoke in the past—Cared!"

"But I gave you up because you loved another man; you loved a man more worthy than I am. I wouldn't have stood aside if I had felt that the other man was not good enough, that he was a waster and would not make you happy; but I knew Tom better than that. Stick to him, don't ask for too much. Believe always that he loves you, and that he is built of the stuff that keeps straight and true, and so, God bless you, dear!"

He kissed her frankly as a brother might, and sat there watching her up the drive to the house. He did not guess that when she gained the house she slipped in by a garden door and ran up to her own room to indulge in that relief that a woman may ever find when the grief is not too black and too bitter, the relief of tears.

"I am worried about her," Hugh thought to himself; but "her" to him meant Joan, not Marjorie.

When he said, "I am worried about her," he meant that he was worried about Joan. If he said, "She would have liked this," "She" would mean Joan.

"I am worried about her and that blackguard Slotman," he thought. "There is something about that man—snake—toad—something uncanny. She's there; she has money and he's out for money. If I can sit here and tell myself that I have scared Slotman from offending and annoying her again, I am an idiot. When there's money to be gained, a man like

Slotman will want a lot of scaring off it."

A week had passed since Marjorie's visit.

Hugh sent for his housekeeper, Mrs. Morrisey.

"Mrs. Morrisey, I am going to London."

"Oh, Mr. Alston, when the men are—"

"The men are all right. I have to go to London on business."

"Very queer and restless he's been," Mrs. Morrisey thought. "I never known him like it before. When I thought he was in love with that pretty little Miss Linden and wanting to marry her, he was not a bit like he is now. He kept cheerful and smiling, and now; forever on the move. No sooner does he get here than back to London he wants to go."

"Shall you be away for long, sir?"

"I don't know," said Hugh. "Perhaps; perhaps not, I can't say."

"I see. Very good, sir. I'll see to things, of course. And about letters, perhaps you won't want them forwarded as you didn't last time, and—"

"I shall want every letter forwarded, the very hour it arrives," said Hugh quickly.

"Very good, sir. Where shall I send them to?"

"I don't know yet. I'll wire you an address."

Yes, he must go to London. He could not go and watch Joan

at Starden, but he could go to London and watch Mr. Philip Slotman.

"What I'll do is this—I'll have a watch kept on that man. There are private detective chaps who'll do it for me. If he goes down to Starden, I'll be after him hot-foot. And if he does go there to annoy and insult Joan—I'll break his neck!" he added, with cheerful decision.

"And she—she is going to marry another man, a man she doesn't love—she can't love. I know she cannot love." He added aloud: "Joan, you don't love him, my darling, you know you don't. You dared not stay and face me that day. Your words meant nothing. You may think you despise me, but you don't: you want to, my dear, but you can't; and you can't because, thank God, you love me! Oh, fool! Cheer yourself up, slap yourself on the back. It doesn't help you. She may love you as you boast, but she'll never marry you. She wants to hate you, and she'll keep on wanting to hate, and I believe—Heaven help me—that her will is stronger than her heart. But—but anyhow, that brute Slotman shan't worry her while I can crawl about."

He was driven to the station the following morning. And now he was in the train for London.

"I'll find out a firm of detectives and put 'em on Slotman," he thought, "but first I'll go and have a look round. What's the name of the place?—Gracebury."

At the entrance to Gracebury, which as everyone knows is a cul-de-sac of no considerable extent, Hugh stopped his taxi and got out. He walked down the wide pavement till he came to the familiar door.

"I'll see him," he thought. "I'll go in and have a few words with him, just to remind him that his neck is in jeopardy."

He went up the stone steps and paused.

The door of Mr. Philip Slotman's office was closed. On the door was pasted a paper, stating that a suite of three offices was to let.

# CHAPTER XXIX

## "WHY DOES SHE TAKE HIM FROM ME?"

"Why—why—why?" Ellice asked herself. Why should this woman who did not love him wish to take him away from her, who worshipped the ground he trod on, who looked up to him as the best, the finest of all God's created creatures?

That Joan Meredyth did not love John Everard no one understood more clearly than Ellice Brand. She had watched them when they were together, she had watched the girl apart; and the watcher's body might be that of a child, but her eyes were the eyes of a woman, as was her heart too.

"Why should she take him from me?" she asked herself, and all her being rose in passionate revolt and resentment.

"Perhaps she does not know that I love him. Perhaps she looks on me only as a child—a silly, foolish, infatuated child. But I am not! I am not!" Ellice cried. "I am not! I love him. I loved him when I was a baby, when I came here eight years ago, and now I am eighteen and a woman, and I have never changed and never shall!"

During the days that followed the announcement of Joan Meredyth's engagement to John Everard, Connie watched the girl. She felt troubled, anxious, and yet scarcely could say why. She knew the girl's passionate nature. Connie almost dreaded something reckless even tragic. She was more worried than she could say and of course she could not consult Johnny. There was no one to consult but Helen, and Helen did not understand Ellice in the least. Helen was inclined to look down on Ellice from her superior height as a wayward, wilful, foolish child—nothing more.

"Send her away. I suppose she is really too old to go to school now, Connie. How old is she, sixteen?"

"Eighteen."

"She has the heart and the body of a child."

"And the soul of a woman!"

"Sometimes, Connie dear," said Helen sweetly, "you make me almost angry. You actually seem to be siding with this foolish little thing!"

Connie sighed. "In—in some ways I do. She loves him so, and I know it. I can't be hard-hearted, I can't blind myself to the truth. Of course, I know that Johnny's marriage with Joan is the best thing in the world for both of them, but—"

"But just because a stupid, self-willed girl of eighteen believes herself deeply in love with Johnny—Oh, Connie, do be your own reasonable self."

Johnny Everard, blind as most men are, did not notice how quiet and reserved Ellice had grown of late, how seldom she spoke to him, how when he spoke to her she only answered him in brief monosyllables, and how never came a smile now to her red lips, and certainly never a smile into her great dark eyes.

He did not see what Connie saw—the heaviness about those eyes, the suggestion of tears during the night, when she came down silently to her breakfast. She had changed, and yet he did not see it, and if he had seen it might never guess at the cause.

And Connie too, always kindly and gentle, always sweet and unselfish; during these days the girl's unselfishness was something to wonder at.

She had always loved Ellice; she had understood the child as none other had. And now there seemed to be a bond between them that drew them closer.

Three years ago Johnny had bought a bicycle for Ellice. She had been going daily then to Miss Richmond's school at Great Langbourne, three miles away, and he had bought the bicycle that she might ride to school and back again. Since she had left school the bicycle had remained untouched and rusted in one of the outhouses, but now Ellice had got the machine out and cleaned it and put new tyres on it.

Deep down in her mind was a plan, as yet not wholly formed, a desperate venture that one day she might embark on, and the old bicycle was part of that plan, for she would need it to carry out the plan. She had not decided yet, not even if she would ever carry it out, but she might.

Day after day saw her on the road; more often than not her way lay towards Starden village. She would ride the six and a half miles to Starden, wait there for a time, and then ride back. She never called at Starden Hall. Helen knew nothing of these trips.

Connie watched the girl with misgivings and doubts, and Ellice knew that the elder girl was watching her.

"Connie, I want to speak to you," she said quietly one morning.

"Yes, darling?"

Ellice slipped her small brown hand into Connie's.

"I—I know that you are worrying, dear, that you are anxious—and for me."

Connie nodded, tears came into her eyes.

"I want you to understand, Connie, that I—I promise you I will do nothing—nothing, I will never do anything unless I come to you first and tell you. I promise you that I will do nothing—nothing that I should not do, nothing mad and foolish and wrong, unless I come to you first and tell you just what I am going to do."

"Thank you, dear, for telling me this. It lifts a great weight and a great anxiety from my heart. Thank you, dear—oh, Ellice darling, I thought once that it would be a fine thing for him, but now—now I could wish it otherwise!"

Another moment and the girl was in her arms, clasping her passionately, and kissing her passionately and gratefully.

Then suddenly Ellice broke away, and a few minutes later was riding hard down the road to Starden.

It was always to Starden that she rode. Always she passed the great gates of Starden Hall, yet never even glanced at them. She rode into the little village, propped her bicycle against the railings that surrounded the old stocks that stood on the village green, and there sat on a seat and watched the ducks in the green village pond and the children playing cricket. Then, after waiting perhaps an hour, she would mount and ride slowly back to Buddesby again.

It was the programme that she carried out this morning. It was twelve o'clock when she came in sight of Buddesby village, a mile distant as yet.

"Missy! Missy!" Someone was calling. Ellice slowed down and looked about her. On the bank beside the road a man sat, and he was nursing an ugly yellow lurcher dog in his arms.

"Missy!" the man called, and his voice was broken and harsh with suffering.

It was Rundle, the poacher, and his dog, and there was blood on Rundle's hand, blood trickling down from a wound in the dog's side. The man was holding the dog as he might have held a child. The big ugly yellow head was against the man's breast, and in its agony the dog was licking the man's rough hand.

And watching, there came back to Ellice's memory what she had said of this man and his dog.

"You'll do something for me, missy, something as I—I can't do myself!" He shuddered. "Will you ride on to Taylor's and ask him to come here and bring—his gun?"

"Why?"

"I—I can't do it myself!"

"He might be cured."

"There's only Mister Vinston, the Vet, and he wouldn't look at this poor tyke of mine. He hates him too bad for that, because Snatcher killed one of them fancy poodle dogs of his two years ago; and Mr. Vinston ain't never forgot it—and never will. He wouldn't do nothing to save Snatcher, miss. Ask Taylor to come and bring his gun."

Ellice nodded. She stretched out her hand and touched the shaggy yellow head, and in her eyes was infinite pity. Then she mounted the bicycle, and rode like the wind to Buddesby. What she said to Mr. Ralph Vinston, the smart young veterinary surgeon, only she and Mr. Ralph Vinston knew.

He had refused definitely and decidedly. "It'll be a blessing to the place if the beast dies," he said. "You'd better take his message to Taylor. The gun's the best remedy for Rundle's accursed dog, Miss Ellice."

And then the girl had talked to him, had talked with flashing eyes and heaving breast, and the end of it was that Ralph Vinston made a collection of surgical instruments, bandages, and other necessaries, bundled them into his little car, and was away down the road with Ellice in company within ten minutes.

# CHAPTER XXX

## "WAITING"

Hugh Alston had certainly not attempted anything in the way of picturesque disguise. There was nothing brigandish or romantic about the appearance of the very ordinary-looking young man who put in an appearance at Starden village.

Quite what his plans were, what he proposed doing and how he should do it, Hugh had not the slightest idea. He mistrusted Slotman. He experienced exactly the same feelings as would a man who, hearing that there was a savage wild beast let loose where an immense amount of harm may be done, puts a gun under his arm and sallies forth.

Even if Joan had not the immense claim on him that she had, he believed he would do exactly what he was doing now. He might be wrong about Slotman, of course. The man might have cleared out and left the country, but Hugh fancied that he had not. Here was a little gold-mine, a young girl, rich and unprotected, a girl of whom this villain believed certain things, which if true would give him a great power over her. That they were not true, Slotman did not know, and he would use his fancied knowledge to obtain his ends and to make Joan's life unbearable.

So Hugh Alston was here in rough, shaggy tweeds, sitting on the self-same seat beside the old stocks where most mornings Ellice Brand came.

"I'm here," he said to himself, and pulled hard on his pipe. "I am here, and here I am going to stay. Sooner or later, unless I am dead out in my reckonings, that brute will turn up, and when he does he'll find me here ahead of and waiting for him."

"The Meredyths," said Mrs. Bonner, "hev lived at Starden"—she called it 'Sta-a-arden'—"oh, I wouldn't like to say for how long, centuries anyhow. Then for a time things got despirit with them, and the place was sold. Bought it was by Mr. Gorridge, a London gentleman. Thirty years he lived here. I remember him buying it; I would be about eighteen then, just before I married Bonner. Master Roger I think it was, anyhow one of 'em—the Meredyths I mean—went to Australia and kep' sheep or something there, and made money, and he bought the old place back, Mr. Gorridge being dead and gone. You'll see 'is tomb in the church, Mr. Alston."

"Thank you," Hugh said. "I'll be sure to look for it."

"A wonderful expensive tomb, and much admired," said Mrs. Bonner.

"I am sure it must be in the best taste. And then?"

"Oh, then Mr. Roger died at sea and left it all, Starden Hall and his money, to Miss Joan Meredyth. And she lives there now, and I suppose she'll go on living there when she is married."

"When she is married," he repeated.

"To Mr. John Everard of Buddesby, a rare pleasant-spoken, nice gentleman as no one can speak a word against. Passes here most days in his car, he does—always running over from Buddesby, as is but natcheral."

Starden Hall gates stood about a quarter of a mile out of Starden village, and midway between the village and the Hall gates was Mrs. Bonner's clean, typically Kentish little cottage.

Artists were Mrs. Bonner's usual customers. The cottage was old, half-timbered and hipped-roofed. The roof was clad with Sussex stone, lichen-covered, and a feast of colour from grey and vivid yellow to the most tender green. Mrs. Bonner herself was a comfortable body, built on ample and generous lines, a born house manager, a born cook, and of a cleanliness that she herself described as "scrutinous."

So Hugh, casting about for a retreat, had happened on Mrs. Bonner's cottage and had installed himself here—for how long he knew not, for what purpose he scarcely even guessed at. Yet here he was.

Mrs. Bonner had seen Philip Slotman, as she saw most things and people that at one time or another passed within range of her windows.

She recognised him from Hugh's description.

"It would be about best part of a fortnight ago," she said. "He had shammy leather gloves on, and was in Hickman's cab. Hickman waited for him at the hall gates and then took him back."

"And he's not been here since?"

"I fancy, but I ain't sure, that I did see him one day in a car," said Mrs. Bonner; "but I couldn't swear to it."

Twice he had seen "Her" from the window of Mrs. Bonner's little cottage, once a mere glimpse as she had flashed by in a car; the other time she had been afoot, walking and alone. He had gazed on the slim grace of her figure, himself hidden behind Mrs. Bonner's spotless white lace curtains. He had watched her, his soul in his eyes, the woman he loved and who was not for him, could never be for him now, and there fell upon him a sense of desolation, of loneliness, of utter hopelessness.

Three days had passed since his coming to Starden. He had seen Joan twice, he had seen the man she was to marry. Once he had caught a glimpse of John Everard hurrying to Starden Hall in his little car, he himself had been standing by Mrs. Bonner's gate. Everard had turned his head and glanced at him, with that curiosity about strangers that all dwellers in rustic places feel.

"An artist, I suppose," Johnny thought as he drove on.

Hugh watched him down the road; he had seen Everard's glance at him, and had summed him up. The man was just what he would have imagined, a man of his own stamp, no Adonis—just an ordinary, healthy, clean-living Englishman.

"I rather like the look of him," thought Hugh. "He seems all right." And then he smiled at his thoughts a trifle bitterly. "By every right on earth I ought to hate him."

Johnny drove his small car to the doors of the Hall.

"Joan," he said, "come out. Come out for a spin—the car's running finely to-day. Come out, and we'll go and have lunch at Langbourne or somewhere. What do you say?" His face was eager. "You know," he added, "you have never been out with me in my car yet."

"If you would like me to."

"Go and get ready then, and I'll tell Helen," he said. "We shan't be back to lunch."

Hugh had been on his way to the village when he saw Everard in his little car. He went to the village because, if he went in the opposite direction, it would take him to the Hall gates, and he did not wish to go there. He did not wish her to see him, to form the idea that he was here loitering about for the purpose of seeing her.

Sooner or later he knew she must be made aware of his presence, then he hoped for an opportunity to explain, but he would not seek it yet. So he made his way to the village, stopped to give pennies to small white-haired children, patted the shaggy dusty heads of vagrant dogs, and finally came to anchor on the seat beside the railed-in stocks.

And there on that same seat sat a small, dark-eyed maiden, whose rusty bicycle reclined against the railings. She had been here yesterday for fifteen minutes or so. He and she had occupied the seat without the exchange of a word, according to English custom.

Hugh looked at her. Because he regarded one woman as the embodiment of all that was perfect and graceful and beautiful, it did not blind him to beauty in others. He saw in this girl what those blinder than he had not yet recognised— the dawning of a wonderful, a radiant and glowing beauty. And because he had a very sincere and honest appreciation of the beautiful, she interested him, and he smiled. He lifted his hat.

The girl stared at him; she started a little as he raised his hat. She gave the slightest inclination of her head. It was not encouraging.

Hugh sat down. He was thinking of the man he had seen a while ago—a clean, honest, open-faced man, a man he felt he could like, and yet by every reason ought to hate.

The girl was studying his profile.

She had the suspicion that is inherent in all shy wild things, and yet, looking at him, she felt that this man was no dangerous animal to be feared and avoided.

Turning suddenly, he caught her glance and smiled.

"You live here?"

"No!"

"Yet you—oh, I see, you are staying here—"

"No, I live at Little Langbourne."

He smiled, having no idea where Little Langbourne might be.

They talked—of nothing, of the ducks and geese on the green, of the weather, of the sunshine, of the ancient stocks.

"You are staying here?" she asked.

"Yes, at Mrs. Bonner's."

"Oh, then you are an artist?"

"Nothing so ornamental, I am afraid. No—quite a useless person."

"If you are not an artist, and have no friends here, do you not find it a little dull?"

"Yes, but I am a patient animal. I am waiting, you see."

"Waiting—for what?"

Hugh smiled. "For something that may happen, and yet may not. I am waiting in case it does. Of course you don't understand, little girl, I—I mean—I am sorry," he apologised. "I was forgetting, thinking of a friend, another girl I know."

"I am not offended. Why should I be? I am a girl and—and not very big, am I?" She rose and smiled at him, and held out her hand.

"Thank you," Hugh said. He took her hand and held it. "I think you are generous."

"For not being offended by a silly thing like that!" She laughed and turned to get the bicycle. But it had slipped, the handle-bar had become wedged in the railings; it took all Hugh's strength to persuade the handle-bar to come out.

"I am afraid you can't ride it like this, the bar's got twisted. If you have a spanner—"

"I haven't," said Ellice.

"Then if you will permit I will wheel it into the village.

There's a cycle shop there, and I'll fix it up for you."

So, he wheeling the bicycle, and she beside him, they crossed the green and came to the village street. And down the road came a little grey-painted car, which Johnny Everard was driving with more pride than he had ever experienced before.

"Why, hello!" thought Johnny. "What on earth is Ellice doing here, and who is the fellow she is with? He's the man I saw at Mrs. Bonner's gate and—"

He turned his head and glanced at Joan. He was going to say something to her, something about the unexpectedness of seeing Ellice here, but Johnny Everard said nothing. He was startled, for Joan's face was white, and her lips were compressed. And in Joan's brain was dinning the question. "He here—what does he do here? Has he come here to torment me further, to pester and plague and annoy me with his speeches that I will never listen to? How dare he come here?"

He had seen her, had paused. He lifted his hand to his hat and raised it, but Joan stared straight before her.

It was the cut direct, and there came a dusky red into Hugh's face as he realised the fact.

# CHAPTER XXXI

## "IF YOU NEED ME"

Naturally enough, Johnny Everard, seeing Ellice, would have stopped. He had his foot on the clutch and was feeling for the brake when Joan realised his intention.

"Please drive on! Please drive straight on!"

And Johnny, receiving his instructions, obeyed them without hesitation. Another moment, and Joan regretted. But it was too late, the car had gone on; the two figures, the man and the girl with the bicycle, were left behind. It was too late—and the girl felt almost shocked by what she had done.

But Joan's temper was on edge, the day had lost any beauty that it might have held for her. She wanted to get back, she wanted to be alone, she wanted to decide, to think things out for herself.

Johnny looked at her. This was beyond his understanding. What had happened? Was it the man who had caused Joan to look so white and angry, or was it Ellice?

It could hardly be the man after all, for she had evidently not known him. She had not recognised him in any way.

Johnny was not good at guess-work. Here was something beyond him. If it were Ellice, then why should the sight of Ellice upset Joan? And why—it came to him suddenly—had Joan cut Ellice?

For in cutting the man Joan had also cut the girl, and had not thought, the girl meaning little or nothing to her.

"Johnny, I—I—don't think me unkind—or ungracious— but—I would like to go back soon. I don't mean—" She paused. "Let's go back by way of Bennerden."

It meant that she did not want to go back by the same road with the chance of seeing those two again.

Ellice's cheeks were burning, and her eyes were bright with anger. Joan Meredyth had cut her, and it seemed to her that Johnny had aided and abetted.

Then she happened to glance at Hugh Alston, and intuition prompted her.

"I think you know her," she said quickly.

"Yes, I—I know her."

"And she was not pleased to see you?"

"Apparently not!" he laughed, but the laughter was shaky. "Here we are! We'll soon get the bicycle fixed up."

Ellice stood watching him while with a borrowed spanner he adjusted the handle-bars.

What did this man know of Joan, and why had Joan cut him dead? Perhaps they were old lovers, perhaps a thousand things? Ellice shrugged her shoulders. It was nothing to her. If she must fight this woman, this rich, beautiful woman for her love's sake, she would not fight with underhand weapons. There would be no digging in pasts, for Ellice.

"Thank you," she said. "You have been very kind!" Again she held out her hand to him, and gave him a frank and friendly smile. "I hope that we shall meet again."

"I think," he said, "that we shall often meet again."

He stood and watched the graceful little figure of her as she sped swiftly down the road, then turned and walked slowly back towards Mrs. Bonner's cottage.

So Joan had seen him, and had cut him dead.

"If I was not so dead sure, so dead certain sure that Slotman will turn up eventually, I would clear out," Hugh thought to himself. "I'd go back to Hurst Dormer and stick there, whether I wanted to or not."

Ellice, pedalling homeward, went more slowly now she was clear of the village. She wanted to think it all over in her mind, and arrived at conclusions. At first she had thought that Joan Meredyth and Johnny too had deliberately cut her dead. But that was folly; they had cut her, but then in this matter she had not counted. She was gifted with plenty of common-sense. Connie's teaching and precept had not gone for nothing with the girl.

"Joan Meredyth knows that man, and he knows her."

Half a mile out of Little Langbourne, Ellice put on the brake and alighted.

"How is Snatcher?" she asked.

Rundle touched his hat. A big and fearsome-looking man was Rundle. Village mothers frightened small children into good behaviour by threatening them that Rundle would come and take them away—a name to conjure with. Little Langbourne only knew peace and felt secure when Rundle was undergoing one of his temporary retirements from activity, when, as a guest of the State, he cursed his luck and the gamekeepers who had been one too many for him.

But there was nothing fearsome about the Rundle who faced little Ellice Brand. There was a smile on the man's lips, in his eyes a look of intense gratitude.

Ragged and disreputable person that he was, he would have lain down and allowed this little lady to wipe her feet on him, did she wish it.

"How is Snatcher?"

"Fine, missy!" he said. "Fine—fine!" His eyes glistened. "Snatcher's going to pull through, missy. 'Twas a car did hit he," he added, "and I saw the chap who was in it. I saw him, and I saw him laugh when Snatcher went rolling over in the dust. I'll watch out for that man, missy."

"Tell me about Snatcher!"

"Leg broke, and a terrible cut from a great flint; but he'll pull through—thanks to you!"

"To Mr. Vinston, you mean!"

Rundle shook his head. "To you. He wouldn't 'a come for me, nor Snatcher; he hates my poor tyke. But he's put

Henry St. John Cooper

Snatcher right for all that, and because you made him do it, and I don't wonder!" Rundle looked at her. "I don't wonder," he added. "There's be few men who wouldn't do what you'd tell 'em to."

"Now," said Ellice, "you are talking absurdly. Of course I just shamed Mr. Vinston into doing it. I'd like to come and see Snatcher, Rundle."

"The queen wouldn't be as welcome," he said simply.

Helen expressed no surprise at the unseasonable return of Joan and Johnny from their trip. There was no accounting for Joan's moods; the main and the great thing was, it was due to no quarrel between them.

Johnny stayed to lunch. After it, Joan left him with Helen and went to her own room. She wanted to be alone, she wanted to think things out, to decide how to act, if she were to act at all.

"He called me ungenerous—three times," she said, "ungenerous and—and now I know that I am, I deserve it." She felt as a child feels when it has done wrong and longs to beg for forgiveness. In spite of her pride, her coldness and her haughtiness, there was much of the child still in Joan Meredyth's composition—of the child's honesty and the child's frankness and innocence and desire to avoid hurting others.

"It was cruel—it was cowardly. But why is he here? What right has he to come here when I—I told him—when he knows—that I, that Johnny and I—"

And now, with her mind wavering this way and that way, anxious to excuse herself and blame him one moment, condemning herself the next, Joan took pen and paper and wrote hurriedly.

"I am sorry for what I did. It was inexcusable, and it was ungenerous. I ask you to forgive me, it was so unexpected. Perhaps I have hurt myself by doing it more than I hurt you. If I did hurt you, I ask your forgiveness, and I ask you also, most earnestly, to go, to leave Starden."

She would have written more, much more, words were tumbling over in her brain. She had so much more to say to him, and yet she said nothing. She signed her name and addressed the letter to Hugh Alston at Mrs. Bonner's cottage. She took it out and gave it to a gardener's boy.

"Take that letter and give it the gentleman it is addressed to, if he is there. If he is not there, bring it back to me."

"Yes, miss." The boy pocketed the letter and a shilling, and went whistling down the road.

So she had written, she had confessed her fault and asked for forgiveness—that was like Joan. One moment the haughty cold, proud woman, the next the child, admitting her faults and asking for pardon.

The letter had been duly delivered at Mrs. Bonner's cottage, and, coming in later, Hugh found it.

"Bettses' Bob brought it," said Mrs. Bonner. "From Miss Meredyth at the Hall," she added, and looked curiously at Hugh.

"That's all right, thanks!"

Mrs. Bonner quivered with curiosity. Who was this lodger of hers who received letters from Miss Meredyth, when he had not even admitted that he knew her?

"Very funny!" thought Mrs. Bonner.

Hugh read the letter. "I am sorry—for what I did.... I ask you to forgive me.... Perhaps I have hurt myself more than I have hurt you ..."

"Any answer to go back to the Hall?"

"None!"

"Ah!" Mrs. Bonner hesitated. "I didn't know you knew Miss Meredyth."

"I am going out," said Hugh. Avoid Mrs. Bonner while she was in this curious mood, he knew he must.

"If there's one thing I can't abide, it is secretiveness," said Mrs. Bonner, as she watched him up the road towards the village.

Should he answer the letter? Hugh wondered. Or should he just accept it in silence, as an apology for an act of rudeness? He hated that idea. She might think that he did not forgive, that he bore malice and ill-will.

"No, I must answer it," he decided, "but what shall I say?" He knew what he wanted to say, he knew that he wanted to ask her to meet him, and he knew only too well that she would refuse.

"There is no sense," said Hugh deliberately, "no sense whatever in riding for a certain fall." He was staring at a small flaxen-haired, dirty-faced boy as he spoke. The boy grinned at him.

"You have a sense of humour," said Hugh, "and, no doubt, a sweet tooth." He felt in his pocket for the coin that the Starden children had grown to expect from him. The boy took it, yelled and whooped, and sped down the street to the sweetstuff shop.

"But the fact remains," said Hugh to himself, "there is no sense in deliberately riding for a fall. If I asked her to meet me, she would either refuse or ignore the request, so I shall not ask. Yet, all the same, she and I will meet sooner or later, and when we meet, it will be by accident, not by—" He paused. Outside the cycle-shop stood a small two-seater car that had a familiar look to Hugh. As he glanced at the car its owner came out of the shop with a can of petrol in his hand.

He saw Hugh, looked him in the eyes, and nodded in friendly fashion.

"A nice day!" he said.

"Very!"

"I have to thank you for helping my—" Johnny paused; he had almost said sister, but of course Ellice was not his sister—"my little friend yesterday, about the bike I mean."

"That's nothing! Excuse interference on my part, but if you pour that petrol into the radiator, you will probably develop trouble."

Johnny Everard laughed. "I am new to it, and I am always doing odd things like that. Of course, that's for water. Lawson over at Little Langbourne generally sees to things for me."

Hugh nodded. He looked at the man standing but a few feet from him, the man who was to gain that which Hugh coveted and desired most in the world, looked at him and yet felt no dislike, no great enmity, no furious hate.

"It was very good of you to help the kiddie with her bike," said Johnny, as he splashed the petrol into the tank. "If you find yourself at any time over at Little Langbourne, we'd be glad to see you. My name's Everard, my place is Buddesby."

"Thanks! It is very good of you, and I shan't forget!" He nodded, smiled, and walked on, then glanced back. He could see Johnny fumbling with the car, and he smiled.

"That's my hated rival, and he seems a decent sort of chap."

An hour later he was back at Mrs. Bonner's cottage.

"The post's come in since you went, Mr. Alston," said Mrs. Bonner, "and there's a letter for you."

It was a bulky envelope from Hurst Dormer. There was a note from Mrs. Morrisey, to say that everything was going as it should go, and she enclosed all the letters that had come by post.

And the first letter that Hugh opened was one on pink paper, delicately scented. How well he remembered that scent! How it brought back to him a certain pretty little face, and a pair of sweet blue eyes.

"Dear little maid," he said. He read the letter, and stared at it in astonishment and dismay.

# CHAPTER XXXII

## THE SPY

It seemed to Hugh Alston that he had not read the letter aright; it was so amazing, so disconcerting, that he felt bewildered. What on earth is wrong? he thought, then he took the letter to the better light at the window and read again.

"MY DEAR HUGH,

"I have been over to Hurst Dormer three times in the car, each time hoping and praying that I might find you; but you are never there now, so I am writing, Hugh, hoping that you will get my letter. I know I have no right to." (This, Hugh noticed, had been carefully crossed out.) "I want to see you so much. I want to ask your advice and help. I don't know what to do, and I am so unhappy, so wretched. Forgive me, dear, for troubling you, but if—if only I could see you I am sure you would help me, and tell me what it is right I should do. Ever and ever

"Your loving,
"MARJORIE."

"So unhappy, so wretched!" Hugh read, and it was this that

Henry St. John Cooper

had amazed him. Here was a girl engaged to be married to the man she loved, the man she had told him she could not live without, the man of her own choice, of her own heart—he himself smoothed the way for her, had taken away his own undesirable person, had stepped aside, leaving the field to his rival, and now ...

Hugh blinked at the letter. "What on earth should she be unhappy about? She has had a quarrel with Tom perhaps, and she wants me to go and talk to him like a Dutch Uncle. Poor little maid! I daresay it is all about twopence! But it seems very real and tragic to her." Hugh sighed. He ought to stay here. This was his place, watching and keeping guard and ward for Joan, yet Marjorie wanted him.

"I'll go. I can be there and back in a couple of days. I'll go."

He had just time to write and catch the early outward mail from Starden, to-day was Thursday.

"MY DEAR MARJORIE,

"I have had your letter, and it has worried me not a little. I can't bear to think of you as unhappy, little girl. I shall come back to Hurst Dormer, and shall be there to-morrow, Friday, early in the afternoon. Send me a wire to say if you will come, or if you would rather that I came to Cornbridge.

"At any rate, be sure that if you are in any trouble or difficulty, or are worried and anxious, you have done just the right thing in appealing for help to

"Your old friend,
"HUGH."

He rang the bell for Mrs. Bonner.

"Mrs. Bonner, I find I am obliged to go away for a time."

"You mean—"

"No," he said, "I don't. I mean that my absence will be temporary. I can't say exactly how long I shall be away, but in the meantime I would like to keep my rooms here."

Mrs. Bonner's face cleared. "Oh yes," she said, "ezackly, I see!"

"I shall run up to Town to-night, and I will write you or wire you when you may expect me back. It may be a week, it may be less; anyhow, I shall come back."

"I am very glad to hear that, Mr. Alston," said Mrs. Bonner heartily.

"I shan't take many things with me, just enough for the night. I'll go and pack my bag, and clear off to catch the six o'clock up train."

Why not go down to Hurst Dormer to-night, and send off this letter to Marjorie from Town instead of posting it here? He could see to a few things in Hurst Dormer on the morrow, see Marjorie, arrange her little troubles and then be back here by Saturday; but as he was not sure of his movements he left it that he would wire Mrs. Bonner his probable time of returning.

"One thing, I'll be able to have a good clear-up when he's gone," Mrs. Bonner thought. Forever her thoughts turned in the direction of soap and water. The temporary absence of anyone meant to Mrs. Bonner an opportunity for a good clean, and she had already started one that very evening when there came a tapping on her door.

"Now, whoever is that worriting this time of the night?" With sleeves rolled up over bare and plump arms she went to the door.

"Oh, good evening, Mrs. Bonner. I 'eard about you losing your lodger."

Mrs. Bonner stared into the darkness.

"Oh, it's you!" Judging by the expression of her voice, the visitor was not a favoured one.

"Yes, it's me!"

"Well, what do you want, Alice Betts?"

"Oh, nothing. I thought I'd just call in friendly-like."

"Very good of you, only I'm busy cleaning up."

"Men do make a mess, don't they? Fancy 'is going off like that. I wonder if the letter had anything to do with it?"

"Letter?"

"Yes, the one Miss Joan give our Bob to bring 'im this afternoon."

"Ha!" said Mrs. Bonner. "I shouldn't be surprised."

"Nor should I. I wonder what he is to her, don't you?"

"No, I don't. I ain't bothered my head thinking. It ain't none of my business, Alice Betts."

Alice Betts giggled.

"Well, any'ow he's gone," she said, and Mrs. Bonner did not contradict her. "And gone sudden."

"Very!"

"Depend on it, it was the letter done it. Well, I won't be keeping you."

"No, I ain't got no time for talking," said Mrs. Bonner, and closed the door. "A nosey Parker if ever there was one! Always shoving 'er saller face where she ain't wanted. I can't abide that gel!"

Miss Alice Betts hurried off to the Bettses' cottage in Starden.

"I got a letter to write in a 'urry. Give me a paper and envelope," she demanded.

"MISTER P. SLOTMAN, Dear sir," Alice wrote. "This is to imform you, as agreed, that Mister Alston has gone. Miss Jone writ him a letter, what about cannot say, only as soon as he gets it, he packs up and leaves Starden. I have been to Mrs. Bonner's to make sure and find it is correck, him having packed up and gone to London. So no more at present from yours truely, MISS ALICE BETTS."

And this letter, addressed to Mr. P. Slotman at the new address with which he had furnished her, went out from Starden by the early morning mail.

After Mrs. Bonner's comfortable but restricted cottage, it was good to be back in the spacious old rooms of Hurst Dormer. Hugh Alston was a home man. He had wired Mrs. Morrisey, and now he was back. To-night he slept once again in his own bed, the bed he had slept in since boyhood.

The following morning brought a telegram delivered by a shock-headed village urchin.

"I will be with you and so glad to see you on Saturday—MARJORIE."

Saturday, and he had hurried so that he might see her to-day.

It was not till late Saturday afternoon that Marjorie came at last, and Hugh had been fuming up and down, looking for her since early morning. Yet if he felt any ill-temper at her delay it was gone at a sight of the little face, so white and woebegone, so frankly miserable and unhappy that his heart ached for the child.

"Oh, Hugh, it is so good to see you again."

He kissed her. What else could he do? And then, holding her hand and drawing it through his arm, he led her into the house. He rang the bell for tea, for it was tea-time when she came.

"You are going to have a good tea first, then you are going to tell me all your troubles, and we are going to put them all straight and right. And then—then, Marjorie, you are going to smile as you used to."

A faint smile came to her lips, her eyes were on his face. "Oh, Hugh, if—if you knew how—how good it is to see you again and hear you speak to me."

He put his hand on her shoulders.

"It is always good to me to see you," he said softly. "You're one of the best things in my world, Marjorie, little maid."

She bent her head, so that her soft cheek touched his hand, and what man could draw his hand away from that caress? Not Hugh Alston.

And now came Phipps with the tea, which he arranged on the small table and retired.

"It's all right between them two," he announced in the kitchen a little later. "She'll be missus here after all, I'll lay ten to one."

"Law bless and save us!" said cook. "I thought it was off, and she was going to marry young Mr. Arundel."

Ordinarily, Marjorie had the sensible appetite of a young country girl. To-day she ate nothing. She sipped her tea, and looked with great soulful, miserable eyes at Hugh.

"And now, little girl, come, tell me."

"Oh, Hugh, not now. It is so difficult, almost impossible to tell you. I wrote that letter days and days before I posted it, and then I made up my mind all of a sudden to post it, and regretted it the moment after."

"Why?"

She shook her head.

"There is something wrong between you and Tom? Tell me, girlie!"

She was silent for a moment. "There is—everything wrong between Tom and—and me. But it is my—my fault, not his. Oh, Hugh, it is all my fault!"

"How?"

"I—I don't love him!" the girl gasped.

"Eh?" Hugh started. He sat back and stared at her. "Why—you—I—I thought—"

"So did I!" she cried, bursting into tears, "but I was wrong—wrong—all wrong. I didn't understand!" Her breast was heaving, there were sobs in her throat, sobs she fought and struggled against.

The dawn of understanding came to him. He believed he saw. She had fancied herself in love with Tom, and now she knew she was not—how did she know? For the simple reason that she found she was in love with someone else. Now who on earth could it be? he wondered.

"Won't you tell me all about it, dear?"

"I—I can't. Don't ask me—I ought not to have written, I ought not to have come. I wish—I wish I had not. It is my fault, not Tom's; he is good and kind and—and patient with me, and I know I am unkind and cross to him, and I feel ashamed of myself!"

"Marjorie!"

"Yes, Hugh?" She looked up.

"Tell me the truth, dear," he said gravely. "Do you realise that you are not in love with Tom because you know now that you are in love with someone else?"

She did not answer in words, nodding speechlessly.

"Is he a good man, dear?"

"The best in the world, Hugh," she said softly—"the finest, the dearest, and best."

"That's bad!" Hugh thought. "But I might have guessed that she would say that, bless her little heart! Poor Tom!" He sighed. "So, after all, this beautiful muddle I have made of things goes for nothing! Do you care to tell me who he is, Marjorie?"

"Don't ask me—don't ask me! I can't tell you! I wish I hadn't come. I had no right to ask you to—to listen to me. I wish I hadn't written now!"

He came across to her and put his hand on her shoulder. He bent and kissed the bright hair.

"Little girl, remember always that I am your old friend and your true friend, who would help you in every way at any time. I am not of much use, I am afraid; but such as I am, I am at your service, dear, always, always! Tell me, what can I do? How can I help you?"

"Nothing, nothing, you—you can't help me, Hugh!"

"Can I see Tom?"

"No, oh no, you must not!"

"Can I see—the other? Marjorie, does he know? Has he spoken to you—not knowing perhaps of your engagement to Tom?"

She shook her head. "He—he doesn't know anything!"

Silence fell on them.

"Don't think about it any more, you can't help me. Hugh, where have you been all this long time?"

"I have been in Kent, at Starden."

"Is—is that where she—"

"Joan? Yes! she lives there. I have been there, believing I can help her, and I shall help her!"

"You—you love her so?"

"Better than my life," he said quietly, and never dreamed how those four words entered like a keen-edged sword into the heart of the girl who heard them.

She rose almost immediately.

"I am a foolish, silly girl, and—and, Hugh, I want you to forget what I told you. I shall forget it. I shall go back to—to Tom, and I will try and be worthy of him, try and be good-tempered and—all he wants me to be. Good-bye, Hugh!"

It seemed to him that she had changed suddenly, changed under his very eyes; the tenderness and the tears seemed to have vanished. She spoke almost coldly, and with a dignity he had never seen in her before, and then she went with scarce a look at him, leaving him sorely puzzled.

# CHAPTER XXXIII

## GONE

"DEAR JOAN,

"I daresay you will wonder at not having heard from me for so long, but I have been busy. Things have been going from bad to worse with me of late, and I have been obliged to give up the old offices in Gracebury. I often think of the days when we were so much together, as I daresay you do. Naturally I miss you, and naturally I want to see you again. I feel that you seemed to have some objection to my coming to your house. That being so, I wish to consult your wishes in every way, and so I am writing to suggest that you meet me to-morrow, that is Saturday night, on the Little Langbourne Road. I daresay you will wonder why I am so familiar with your neighbourhood, but to tell you the truth I am naturally so interested in you that I have been down quietly several times—motoring, just to look round and hear news of you from local gossip, which is always amusing. I have heard of your engagement, of course, and I am interested; but we will talk of that when we meet—to-morrow night at the gate leading into the field where the big ruined barn stands, about half a mile out of Starden on the Little Langbourne Road at nine o'clock. This is definite and precise, isn't it? It will then be dark enough for you to be unobserved, and you will come. I am sure you will come. You would not anger and pain an old friend by refusing.

"I hear that the happy man is a sort of gentleman farmer who lives at Buddesby in Little Langbourne. If by any chance I should fail to see you at the place of meeting, I shall put up at Little Langbourne, and shall probably make the acquaintance of Mr. John Everard.

"Believe me,
"Your friend,
"PHILIP SLOTMAN."

It was a letter that all the world might read, and see no deep and hidden meaning behind it, but Joan knew better. She read threat and menace in every line. The man threatened that if she did not keep this appointment he would go to Langbourne and find John Everard, and then into John Everard's ears he would pour out his poisoned, lying, slanderous story.

Better a thousand times that she herself should go to Johnny and tell him the whole truth, hiding nothing. Yet she knew that she could not do that; her pride forbade. If she loved him—then it would be different. She could go to him, she could tell him everything, laying bare her soul, just because she loved him. But she did not love him. She liked him, she admired him, she honoured him; but she did not love him, and in her innermost heart she knew why she did not love Johnny Everard, and never would.

But the letter had come, the threat was here. What could she do? to whom turn? And then she remembered that hard by her own gate was a man, the man to whom she owed all this, all her troubles and all her annoyance and shame, but a man who would fight for and protect and stand by her. Her heart swelled, the tears gathered for a moment in her eyes.

He had not answered the letter she had sent him a couple of days ago. She had looked for an answer, and had felt disappointed at not receiving one, though she had told herself that she expected none.

For long Joan hesitated, pride fighting against her desire for help and support. But pride gave way; she felt terribly lonely, even though she was soon to be married to a man who loved her. To that man ought she to turn, yet she did not, and hardly even gave it a thought. She had made no false pretences to Johnny Everard. She had told him frankly that she did not love him, yet that if he were willing to take her without love, she would go to him.

So now, having decided what she would do, Joan went to her room to write a letter to the man she must turn to, the man who had the right to help her. She flushed as the words brought another memory into her mind; the flush ran from brow to chin, for back into her mind came the words the man had uttered. Strange it was how her mind treasured up almost all that he had ever said to her.

*"You gave me that right, Joan, when you gave me your heart!"*

That was what he had said, and she would never forget, because she knew—that it was true.

She went to her own room, where was her private writing-table. She found the room in the hands of a maid dusting and sweeping.

"You need not go, Alice," she said. "I am only going to write a letter." The girl went on with her work.

"I did not think to appeal to you, yet I find I must appeal for help that I know you will give, because but for you I should not need it. I—"

She paused.

"Funny, miss, Mrs. Bonner's lodger going off like that in such a hurry, wasn't it?" said the girl on her knees beside the hearth.

Joan started. "What do you mean, Alice?"

"The gentleman you gave our Bob a letter for—Mr. Alston," said Alice Betts. "Funny his going off like he did in such a hurry."

"Then you—you mean he is gone?"

"Thursday night, miss."

Gone! A feeling of desolation and helplessness swept over Joan.

Gone when she had counted so on his help! She remembered what she had written: "I ask you earnestly to leave Starden," and he had obeyed her. It was her own fault; she had driven him away, and now she needed him.

The girl was watching her out of the corner of her small black eyes. She saw Joan tear up the letter she had commenced to write.

"It was to him, she didn't know he had gone," Alice Betts thought, and Alice Betts was right.

\*   \*   \*   \*   \*

Mr. Philip Slotman had fallen on evil days, yet Mr. Philip Slotman's wardrobe of excellent and tasteful clothes was so large and varied that poverty was not likely to affect his appearance for a long time to come.

Presumably also his stock of cigars was large, for leaning against the gate beside the tumble-down barn he was drowning the clean smell of the earth and the night with the more insinuating and somewhat sickly smell of a fine Havannah.

Some way down the road, perhaps a quarter of a mile distant, stood a large shabby car drawn up against a hedge, and in that car dozed a chauffeur.

Mr. Slotman took out his watch and looked at it in the dim light.

It was past nine, and he muttered an oath under his breath.

"She won't be such a fool as not to come now that fellow's gone!" he thought, and he was right, for a few moments later she was there.

"So you did come?"

"I am here," Joan said quietly. "You wish to speak to me?"

"Don't be so confoundedly hold-off! Aren't you going to shake hands?"

"Certainly not!"

"Oh, very well!" he snarled. "Don't then. Still putting on your airs, my lady!"

"I am here to hear anything you wish to say to me. Any threats that you have to make, any bargain that you wish to propose. I thought when I paid you that money—"

"That money's gone; it went in a few hours."

He felt savagely angry at her calmness, at her pride and superiority. Why, knowing what he knew, she ought to be pretty well on her knees to him.

"Please tell me what you wish to see me about and let me go. It is money, of course?"

Her voice was level, filled with scorn and utter contempt, and it made the man writhe in helpless fury.

"Look here, stow that!" he said coarsely. "Don't ride the high horse with me. Remember I know you, know all about you. I know who you are and what you are, and—and don't—don't"—he was stuttering and stammering in his rage—"don't think you can put me in my place, because you can't!"

Joan did not answer.

"If I want money I've got a right to ask for it! And I do. I've got something to sell, ain't I?—knowledge and silence. And silence is worth a lot, my girl, when a woman's engaged to be married, and when there's things in her past she don't care about people knowing of. Yes, Miss Joan Meredyth, my lady clerk on three quid a week was one person, but Miss Meredyth of Starden Hall, engaged to be married to Mr. John Everard of Buddesby, is another, ain't she?"

"Please say what you have to say," she said coldly. "I do not wish to stay here with you."

"But you are going to," he said. "You are going to!" He reached out suddenly and gripped her hand. He had expected that she might struggle; it would have been human if she had, but she didn't.

"Please release my hand," she said coldly. "I do not wish to stay here with you!" She paused. "Tell me why you wish to see me!"

He dropped her hand with a snarling oath.

"Well, if you want to know, it is money, and this time it is good money. I am up against it, and I've got to have money. I've been down here several times, hunting round, listening to things, hearing things. I heard about your engagement. I have heard about you. Oh, everyone looks up to you round here—Miss Meredyth of Starden!" He laughed. "And it is going to pay Miss Meredyth of Starden to shut my mouth, ain't it? June, nineteen eighteen, ain't so long ago, is it? Mr. Hugh Alston—hang him!—you set him on to me, didn't you?"

"So you have seen him?"

"I saw him, curse him! He came and—and—'

"Thrashed you?" Joan asked quietly "I thought he might!"

"Stop it! Stop your infernal airs!" he almost shouted. "I am here for money, and I want it, and mean to have it—five thousand this time!"

"I shall not pay you!"

"Oh, you won't—you won't! Then I go to Buddesby. I'll have a little chat there. I'll tell them a few things about Marlbury and about a trip to Australia that did not come off, and about a marriage that never took place. I've got quite a lot to chat about at Buddesby, and I shan't be done when I'm through there either. There's a nice little inn in Starden, isn't there? If one talked much there it would soon get about the place!"

Under cover of the darkness her cheeks flamed, but her voice was still as cold and as steady as before.

"Have you ever considered," she asked quietly, "that what you think you know, may not be true?"

"It is true! And if it isn't true, it is good enough for me; but it is true!"

"It is not!"

He laughed. "It is—at any rate I think so, and others'll think so. It'll want a lot of explaining away, Joan, won't it? if even it isn't true. But I know better. Well, what about it—about the money?"

"I shall consider," she said quietly. "I paid you before, blackmail! If I asked you if this was the final payment, and you said Yes. I know that I need not believe you, so—so I shall consider. I shall take time to think it over."

"Oh, you will?"

"Yes!"

Down the road came a cart. It lumbered along slowly, the carter trudging at the horse's head. Slotman looked at the slow-coming figure and cursed under his breath.

"When shall I hear?"

"I shall think it over, decide how I shall act, whether I shall pay you this money or not," she said. "In a few days, this day week, not before." She turned away.

"And—and if I go to Buddesby and get talking?"

"Then of course I pay you nothing!" she said calmly.

That was true. Slotman gritted his teeth. Two minutes later the carter trudging on his way passed a solitary man smoking by a gate, and far down the road a woman walked quickly towards Starden.

Henry St. John Cooper

# CHAPTER XXXIV

## "FOR HER SAKE"

Into Hugh Alston's life had come two women, women he had loved, both now engaged to be married to other men, and Hugh Alston was a sorely worried and perplexed man about both of them.

"I'll go to Cornbridge to-morrow," said Hugh, and he went.

"Where," asked Lady Linden, "the dickens have you been?"

"In the country!"

"Isn't your own country good enough for you?" She looked at him shrewdly. She saw the worry in his face; it was too open and too honest to make concealment of his feelings possible.

Marjorie welcomed him with tearful gladness in her eyes. She said nothing, she held his hand tightly. Not till afterwards did she thank him for coming.

"I felt you would," she said. "I knew you would!"

And so he was glad he came.

And was she? She wondered, better a thousand times for her and her happiness if she never saw him again. So long as she lived she would not forget those four words that had entered like a sword into her heart and had slain for ever the last hope of happiness for her—"Better than my life!"

It was odd how women remembered Hugh Alston's words. How even on this very day another woman was remembering, and was fighting a fight, pride and obstinacy opposed to fear and loneliness and weariness of soul.

Hugh noticed a change in Tom.

"Hello, Alston," said Tom, and gripped him by the hand; but it was a weary and dispirited voice and grip, unlike those of Tom Arundel of yore.

They walked about Lady Linden's model farm together, Tom acting as showman with no little pride, and yet behind even the enthusiasm there was a weariness that Hugh detected.

"And the wedding, Tom?" Hugh asked him presently. "When is it to be?"

Tom looked up. "I don't know, Alston, sometimes I think never. Alston, you—you've seen her. You remember her as she was, the sweetest, dearest girl in the world, her eyes and her heart filled with sunshine, and now..." The lad's voice trailed off miserably.

"Hugh, I can't make her out; it worries me and puzzles me and—and hurts me. She is so different, she takes me up so sharply. I—I know I am a fool, I know I am not fit to touch her little hand. I know that I am not a man—like you, a man a girl could look up to and respect, but I've always loved her, Hugh, and I've kept straight. There are things I might have

Henry St. John Cooper

done and didn't do—for her sake. I just thought of her, Hugh, and so—so I've lived a decent life!"

Hugh's eyes kindled, for he knew that what the boy said was truth.

Thursday afternoon saw Hugh back at Hurst Dormer. It was a week now since he had left Starden. She had asked him to leave, and he had left, yet not exactly for that reason. His coming here had done no good, had only given him fresh worry and anxiety, and now he realised that all his sympathy was for Tom and not for Marjorie.

"Oh, my Lord! Uncertain, coy and hard to please is correct, and I suppose some of them can be ministering angels—yes, God bless them! I've seen them!" His face softened, his thoughts flew back to other days, days of strife and bloodshed, of misery and death, days when men lay helpless and in pain, and in memory Hugh saw the gentle, soft-footed girls at their work of mercy. Ministering angels—God's own!

"Mrs. Morrisey, I am going to London."

"Very good, sir!" Mrs. Morrisey was giving up all hopes of this restless young master of hers. "Very good, sir!"

"I shall be back"—he paused—"eventually, if not sooner!"

"Certainly, sir!" said Mrs. Morrisey, who had no sense of humour.

"Meanwhile, send on any letters to the Northborough Hotel. I shall catch the seven-thirty," said Hugh.

"I'll order the car round, sir," said Mrs. Morrisey.

And this very day at Starden pride broke down; the need was so great. It was not the money that the man demanded, but the bonds that paying it would forge about her, bind her for all time.

"Please come to me here. I want your help. I am in great trouble, and there is no one I can turn to but you.

"JOAN."

And not till after the letter was in the post did she remember that she had signed it with her Christian name only.

# CHAPTER XXXV

## CONNIE DECLARES

"My dear Connie!" Helen Everard was amazed. "My dear Connie, why talk such nonsense? This marriage between Joan and Johnny is the best, the very best possible thing in the world for him. Joan is—"

"I know all she is, Helen," said Connie; "no one knows better than I do. I know she is lovely; she is good, she is rich, and she is cold—cold to Johnny. She doesn't love him; and I love him, Helen, and I hate to think that Johnny should give his life to a woman who does not care for him!"

Helen shrugged her shoulders. "Sometimes, Connie with her queer unworldly notions annoys me," she thought.

"At any rate, dear child, it is all arranged, and whatever you and I say will not matter in the least. But, all the same, I am sorry you are opposed to the marriage."

"I am!" said Connie briefly.

She had declared herself, as she had known sooner or later she must, and she had declared on the side of the girl who loved Johnny Everard better than her life.

At home Johnny wondered at the change that had come to the two women whom he loved and believed in. It seemed to him that somehow they were antagonistic to him, they seemed to cling together.

Ellice deliberately avoided him. When he asked her to go out, as in the old days, she refused, and when he felt hurt Connie sided with her.

"Con, what does it mean?" he cried in perplexity.

"Nothing. What should it mean?"

"But it does. Ellice hardly speaks to me. When I speak to her she just answers. You—you"—he paused—"and you are different even. What have I done?"

"You have done nothing—yet, Johnny. It is what you are going to do—that troubles me and makes me anxious."

He stared, open-eyed.

"How?"

"Your marriage!"

"With Joan. You mean that you are against her?"

"I am against any woman who would have you for a husband and give you none of her heart," cried Connie.

"Why—why?" he stammered. "Con, you couldn't expect that Joan would fall in love with a chap like me?"

"Then why is she going to marry you? Isn't marriage a union of love and hearts? Oh, Johnny, I am anxious, very anxious. I

Henry St. John Cooper

hate it, this loveless marriage—"

"But I love her!" he said reverently.

"Do you—can you go on loving her? Can you? Your own heart starved, can you continue to love and give again and again? No, no, I know better—the time will come when you will realise you have married a cold and beautiful statue, and your heart will wither and shrivel within you, Johnny."

"Con, in time I will make her care for me a little."

"She never will!"

"Why?"

Connie looked out of the window. "Johnny, dear, if I am saying something that will hurt you, will you forgive me?— knowing that I love you so dearly, that all I want to see is your happiness, that I hate to see you imposed on, made a fool of, made a convenience of!"

"Connie, what do you mean?"

"I mean that I believe that Joan Meredyth will never love you, because all the heart she has to give has been given to someone else."

"You have no right to say that. What do you know? What can you know?"

"I know nothing. I can only guess. I can only stumble and grope in the dark. Think! That woman, lovely, sweet, brilliant, could she accept all that you offer her and give nothing in return if she were heart-free? Wouldn't your love for her appeal to her, touch her, force some tenderness in response? Oh, I have watched her. I have seen, and I have guessed what I know must—must be true. For she is all woman; she is no cold icicle, but you have not touched her heart, Johnny, and you never will, and so—so, my dear," Connie's voice choked with a sob, "you'll hate me for this— Johnny!"

He went to her, put his arm about her, and held her tightly and kissed her.

"To prove my hate, dear," he whispered, and then he went out with a very thoughtful look on his face.

In the yard he saw Ellice.

"Gipsy girl," he said, "come with me. Let's go out—anywhere in the car for a ride—it doesn't matter where. Come with me!"

Her face flushed, then paled.

"No thank you!" she said coldly. "I am busy doing something for Joan."

Johnny sighed with disappointment, there was pain in his eyes too. In the old days she would not have refused; she would have come gladly.

"My little Gipsy girl is against me too!" He walked away slowly and dejectedly, and the girl watched him. She lifted her hands and pressed them hard against her breast, and then—then Johnny heard the light fall of swift-moving feet. He felt a clutch on his arm, and turned. He saw a flushed face, bright eyes were looking into his.

"If—if you want me to, I'll come," she said. "I'll come with you—anywhere!"

He did not answer. His hands had dropped on to her shoulders; he stood there holding her and looking into her face, glowing with a beauty that he had never seen in it before, and in his eyes was still that puzzled look, the look of a man who does not quite understand.

"Why, Gipsy girl!" he said slowly, "you are a woman—you have grown up all suddenly."

"Yes, I am—I am a woman!" She laughed, but the laughter ended in a sob. She bent her head, and Johnny, strangely puzzled, slipped his arm about her and drew her a little closer to him.

He had thought her a child; but she was a woman, and he had seen in her eyes that which set his dull wits wondering.

# CHAPTER XXXVI

## "HE HAS COME BACK"

It was exactly a week since his departure that Hugh returned to Starden, and found Mrs. Bonner a little surprised, but by no means unready.

"You said as you'd send me a message, sir," she said.

"I did, and I haven't done it—I'll take the consequences." But there were no consequences to take. She prepared him an ample meal at the shortest notice, and was willing enough to stop and talk to him while he ate it.

"Anything new, anything fresh?"

"Nothing!"

"No strangers about Starden?"

"No!"

Had Slotman been? That was what Hugh wanted to know. Presently he asked the question direct.

"You don't happen to have seen that man I described to you

some time back, a stout man with a lean face, overdressed, thick red lips, small eyes?"

"Law bless us! yes. I see him two days ago, drove past he did in a car—a shabby-looking car it was, but he didn't stop. He just stared at the cottage as he drove past, and I got an idea he smiled, only I ain't sure. I am sure of one thing, however; he did stare terribul hard at this cottage!"

"You are sure it is the man?"

Mrs. Bonner described Mr. Slotman's appearance vividly, and Mr. Slotman, had he been there, might not have been pleased to hear of the impression he had made on the good woman.

"A man," she concluded, "as I wouldn't trust, not a hinch!"

"It's the man!" Hugh thought. "And he's come back, as I thought he would. Funny he should look at the cottage! Good Lord! I wonder if he has spies about here?"

"Anyone else been? I suppose no one came here to ask about me, for instance, Mrs. Bonner?"

"No one, sir, not a soul, no—stay a moment. The day you left that there nosey Parker of a gel Alice Betts came. I couldn't make out whatever she came for. Me, I don't 'old with them Bettses, anyhow she came. It was her brother that brought you that letter from Miss Joan Meredyth the day you went, sir, and she said something about 'earing as I'd lost my lodger."

"I see. And who is Alice Betts?"

"Her—she be a maid at Starden Hall."

"I see," Hugh repeated. "I see! Mrs. Bonner," he said, "will you do something for me?"

"Anything, of course!"

"Will you take a letter for me to Miss Joan Meredyth?"

Would she not? Mrs. Bonner caught her breath. Then there was something between these two, even though Miss Joan Meredyth was engaged to marry Mr. John Everard of Buddesby!

"Mrs. Bonner," said Hugh a few minutes later, "I am going to trust you absolutely. Miss Meredyth and I—are—old friends. It is urgent that I see her. I want you to take this letter to her; tell no one at the Hall that the letter is from me, tell no one that I am back. No one knows. I did not meet a soul on the road from the station, and I don't want my presence here known. I am trusting you!"

"You can, sir!"

"I am sure of it. Take that note to Miss Meredyth, ask to see her personally. Don't mention my name. Give her that letter, and if, when she has read it, she will come with you, bring her here, because I must see her, and to-night."

It was Alice Betts who opened the door to Mrs. Bonner.

"Oh, good evening, Mrs. Bonner!"

"I didn't come 'ere to bandy no words with you," said Mrs. Bonner. "I never held with you, Alice Betts," she added severely.

"I don't see what I've done!"

"No pre-aps you don't. Anyhow, I'm here to see your mistress. You go and tell her I am here."

"If I say I've brought a letter that gel will guess who it is from," Mrs. Bonner thought, so, wisely, she held her peace.

A few minutes later Mrs. Bonner was shewn into the drawing-room. She dropped a curtsey.

"You want to see me?"

"Yes, miss, but first—excuse me, miss!"

Mrs. Bonner hurriedly opened the door.

"I thought so," she said. "Didn't you best be getting off to your work?"

Alice Betts went.

"A spy! If I might make so bold, miss, I'd get rid of her. Them Bettses never was no good, what with the drink and things. I got a letter for you, miss, only I didn't want that gel to know it."

"Joan, I am back again. No one knows that I am, here except Mrs. Bonner and now yourself. I have reasons for wishing my return to remain unknown. But I must see you. You will believe that I would not ask you to come to me here if there was not urgent need."

There was urgent need, and she knew it, for had she not written that appeal to him barely twenty-four hours ago? There had been no delay this time in his coming.

"And he, Mr. Alston, is at your cottage?"

"Yes, miss, came back only about a hour ago, and he's waiting there. He told me maybe you might come back with me, and he's trusting me not to tell anyone he's here, miss."

"Yes, I understand. And, Mrs. Bonner, you think that girl is a spy?"

"I know it. Wasn't she starting to listen at the keyhole and me hardly inside the room?"

Joan was silent for a moment. "Go back! Tell him—I shall come—presently. Tell him I am grateful to him for coming so quickly."

"I'll tell him."

Mrs. Bonner was gone, and Joan sat there hesitating. A trembling fit of nervousness had come to her, a sense of fear, strangely mingled with joy.

"I must go, there is no one else, but—I do not wish to see him," and yet she knew that she did. She wished to see him more than she wanted to see anything on earth. So presently when Helen, who retired early, had gone upstairs, Joan slipped a cloak over her shoulders and stole out of the house as surreptitiously as any maid stealing to a love tryst.

In Mrs. Bonner's tiny sitting-room Hugh was pacing restlessly in the confined space, pausing now and again to listen.

She was coming—coming. Presently she would be here, presently he would see her, this girl of his dreams, standing before him with the lamplight on her sweet face.

But it was not to pour out the story of his love that he had

Henry St. John Cooper

sent for her to-night. He must remember that she came unattended, unprotected, relying on his chivalry. Hugh took a grip on himself, and now he heard the familiar creaking of the little gate, and in a moment was at the door. But the excitement, the enthusiasm of just now was passed.

He looked at her standing before him. Looking at her, he pictured her as he had seen her before, cold and haughty, her eyes hard and bright, her lips curved with scorn for him, and now—he saw her with a flush in her cheeks, and the brightness of her eyes was not cold, but soft and misty, and her red-lipped mouth trembled.

Once he had seen her as now, all sweetness and tenderness. And so in his dreams of her had he pictured her, and now he saw her so again, and knew that his love for her and need of her were greater even than he had believed.

"I sent for you, Hugh." She hesitated, and again the colour deepened in her cheeks.

"You sent for me, dear?"

"Because I need you. I want your advice, perhaps your help. He—he came back again."

"When?"

"Last Saturday."

"And I left here Thursday," he smiled. "Joan, you have a spy in your house who reports my movements and yours to Slotman. No sooner was I gone from here than he was advised, and so he came. Now do you understand why I am here. I knew that man would come. He needs money, there is the magnet of your gold. He will never leave you in peace while he thinks you alone and unprotected, but while I was here you were safe, for he is a very coward."

"And that was why you came, knowing that he—"

She paused. "And I—I cut you in the street, Hugh."

"And hurt yourself by doing it," he said softly.

"Yes." She bowed her head, and then suddenly she thrust the softness and the tenderness from her, for they must be dangerous things when she loved this man as she did, and was promised to another.

"I must not forget that—I am—" She paused.

"Promised to another man? But you will never carry out that promise, Joan—you cannot, my dear! You cannot, because you belong to me. But it was not of that that you came to speak. Only remember what I have said. It is true."

"It cannot be true. I never break a promise! What am I to do? Tell me and advise me. You know—what he—he says— what he thinks or—or pretends to think." Again the burning flush was in her cheeks.

"I know!"

"And even though it is all a vile and cruel lie, yet I could not bear—"

"You shall not suffer!"

"Don't—don't you understand that if people should think— think of such a thing and me—that they should speak of it and utter my name—Lies or truth, it would be almost the same; the shame of it would be horrible—horrible!" She was trembling.

"Tell me, have you seen this man?"

"Yes, last Saturday. He wrote ordering me to meet him. In every line of the letter I read threats. I—I had to go; it was money, of course, five thousand pounds."

"And you didn't promise?" His voice was harsh and sharp, and looking at him she saw a man changed, a man whose face was hard and stern, and whose mouth had grown bitter. And, knowing it was for her, she knew that she had never admired him before as she did now.

"I promised nothing. I am to meet him again to-morrow night and—and tell him what I have decided. It is not the money, but—but to pay would seem as if I—I were afraid. And oh, I have paid before!"

"I know! And to-morrow you will meet him?"

"I—but—"

"You will meet him, Joan, but I shall be there also. Tell me where!"

She described the place, and he remembered it and knew it well enough.

"I shall be there, remember that. Go without fear—answer as you decide, but remember you pay nothing—nothing. And then I,"—he paused, and smiled for the first time—"I will do the paying."

# CHAPTER XXXVII

## THE DROPPING OF THE SCALES

It was like turning back the pages of a well-loved book, a breath out of the past. For this afternoon it seemed to John Everard that his little friend, almost sister, had come back to him.

And yet it seemed to Johnny, who studied her quietly, that here was one whom he had never known, never seen before. The child had been dear to him as a younger sister, but the child was no more.

And to-day, for these few brief hours, Ellice gave herself up to a happiness that she knew could be but fleeting. To-day she would be the butterfly, living and rejoicing in the sun. The darkness would come soon enough, but to-day was hers and his.

How far in his boldness John Everard drove that little car he did not quite realise, but it was a slight shock to him to read on a sign-post "Holsworth four miles," for Holsworth was more than forty miles from Little Langbourne.

"Gipsy, we must go back," he said. "We'll get some tea at the farmhouse we passed a mile back, and then we will hurry on.

Con will be worrying."

They had tea at the little farmhouse, and sat facing one another, and more than ever grew the wonder in Johnny's mind. Why—why had this girl changed so? What was the meaning of it, the reason for it? It was not the years, for a few days, a few short weeks had wrought the change. And then he remembered with a sense of shame and wrongdoing that, strangely enough, he had scarcely flung one thought to Joan all that long afternoon.

And now in the dusk of the evening they set off on the homeward journey. And at Harlowe happened the inevitable, when one has only a small-sized tank, and undertakes a journey longer than the average, the petrol ran out. The car stopped after sundry spluttering explosions and back-firings.

"Nothing else for it, Gipsy. I must tramp back to Harlowe and get some petrol—serves me right, I ought to have thought of it. Are you afraid of being left there with the car?"

"Afraid!" She laughed. "Afraid of what, Johnny?"

"Nothing, dear!"

He set off patiently with an empty petrol tin in each hand, and she watched him till he was lost in the dusk.

"Afraid!" she repeated. "Afraid only of one thing in this world—of myself, of my love for him!" And then suddenly sobs shook her, and she buried her face in her hands and cried as if her heart must break.

It took Johnny a full hour to tramp to Harlowe and to tramp back with the two heavy tins, and then something seemed to go wrong. The car would not start up: another hour passed, and they had a considerable way to go, and then suddenly, seemingly without rhyme or reason, the car started and ran beautifully, and once more they were off and away.

But they were very late when they came into Starden, and with still some six and a half miles to go before they could reassure Connie.

"Connie will be worrying, Gipsy," Johnny said. "You know what Connie is, bless her! She'll think all sorts of tragedies— and—" He paused, his voice faltered, shook, and became silent.

They were running past Mrs. Bonner's cottage. The door of the cottage stood open, and against the yellow light within they could see the figure of a man and of a girl, and both knew the girl to be Joan Meredyth, and the man to be Mrs. Bonner's lodger, the man that Joan had cut that day in Starden.

The car was a quarter of a mile further down the road before either spoke, and then Johnny said, and his voice was jerky and uncertain:

"Yes, Connie will be getting nervous. I shall be glad to have you home—Gipsy."

# CHAPTER XXXVIII

## "HER CHAMPION"

Why should Joan have been at Mrs. Bonner's cottage at such an hour? Why should she have been there talking to the very man whom she had a week ago cut dead in the village? Why, if she had anything to say to him, whoever he was, had she not sent for him rather than seek him at his lodgings?

Questions that puzzled and worried Johnny Everard sorely, questions that he could not answer. Jealousy, doubt, and all the kindred feelings came overwhelmingly. Honest as the day, he never doubted a soul's honesty. If he found out that a man whom he had trusted was a thief, it shocked him; he kicked the man out and was done with him, and nothing was left but an unpleasant memory, but Joan was different.

Trust Joan? Of course he did, utterly and entirely.

"I should be unworthy of her if I didn't," he thought. "In any case, I am not worthy of her. It is all right!"

But was it all right?

Connie had been naturally a little anxious. She, womanlike, had built up a series of tragedies in her mind, the worst of which was Johnny and Ellice lying injured and unconscious on some far distant roadway; the least a smashed and disabled car, and Johnny and Ellice sitting disconsolate on a roadside bank.

But here they were, all safe and sound, and Connie bustled about, hurrying up the long delayed dinner, making anxious enquiries, and feeling a sense of relief and gratitude for their safe return, about which she said nothing at all.

And now Connie was gone to bed, and Ellice too; and Johnny smoked his pipe and frowned over it, and asked himself questions to which he could find no answer.

"But I trust her, absolutely," he said aloud. "Still, if she knows the man"—he paused—"why hasn't she spoken to me about him? I am to be her husband soon, thank Heaven, but—"

And then came more doubts and worries crowding into his mind, and his pipe went out, and he sat there, frowning at thoughts, greatly worried.

Johnny Everard looked up at the sound of the opening of the door. In the doorway stood a little figure. He had never realised how little she was till he saw her now, standing there with her bare feet and a thin white dressing-gown over her nightdress, her hair hanging in great waving tresses about her oval face and shoulders and far down her back.

She looked such a child—and yet such a woman, her great eyes anxiously on his face.

"Johnny," she said softly, "you have been worrying."

He nodded, speechless.

"Why, Johnny?"

"Because—because, Gipsy, I am a fool—a jealous fool, I suppose."

"If you doubt her honour and her honesty, Johnny, then you are a fool," she said bravely, "because Joan could not be mean and treacherous and underhand. It would not be possible for her."

"I thought you did not—like Joan?"

"And does that make any difference? Even if I do not like her, must I be unjust to her? I know she is fine and honourable and true and straight, and you must know that too, so—so why should you worry, Johnny? Why should you worry?"

"Why has she never said one word to me about this man? Why did she refuse to recognise him that day when she saw you and him together? Why does she go to Mrs. Bonner's cottage to meet him late at night?"

He hurled at her all those questions that he had been asking himself vainly.

"I do not know why," Ellice said gravely, "but I know that, whatever the reason is, it is honourable and honest. Joan Meredyth," she paused a little, with a catch of the breath, "Joan Meredyth could not be other than honest and true and—and straight, Johnny. It would not be her nature to be anything else."

"Why do you come here? Why do you come to tell me this, Gipsy?" He had risen, he stood looking at her—such a little thing, so graceful, so lovely with the colour in her cheeks, the light in her eyes, the light of her fine generosity. "Gipsy—" He became silent; looking at her, strange thoughts came—wild, impossible thoughts, thoughts that come when dreams end and one is face to face with reality. So many years he had known her, she had been part and parcel of his life, his everyday companion, yet it seemed to him that he had never known her till now—the fineness, the goodness of her, the beauty of her too, the womanliness of this child.

"I came here to tell you, Johnny, because you let yourself doubt," she said. "I heard you moving about the room restlessly, and that is not like you. Usually you sit here and smoke your pipe and think or read your paper. You never rise and move about the room as to-night."

"How do you know?"

She laughed shortly. "I know—everything," she said. "I listen to you night after night. I always have for years. I have heard you come up and go to your room, always. I always wait for that!"

"Gipsy, why—why should you?"

"Because," she said—"because—" And then she said no more, and would have turned away, her errand done, but that he hastened to her and caught her by the hand.

"Gipsy, wait. Don't go. Why did you come to tell me this of Joan to-night?"

"Because since you have asked her to be your wife, you belong to her, and you should not doubt her. She is above doubt—she could not be as some women, underhand and treacherous, deceitful. That would not be Joan Meredyth."

"And yet you do not like her, dear. Why not?"

"I can't—tell you." She tried to wrench her hand free, yet he held it strongly, and looked down into her eyes.

What did he see there? What tale did they in their honesty tell him, that hers lips must never utter? Was he less blind at this moment than ever before in his life? Johnny Everard never rightly understood.

"Good night," he said, "Gipsy, good night," and would have drawn her to him to kiss her—as usual, but she resisted.

"Please, please don't!" she said, and looked at him.

Her lips were quivering, there was a glorious flush in her cheeks; and in her eyes, a kind of fear. So he let her go, and opened the door for her and stood listening to the soft swish of her draperies as she sped up the dark stairs.

Then very slowly Johnny Everard came back to his chair. He picked up his pipe and stared at it, yet did not see it. He saw a pair of eyes that seemed to burn into his, eyes that had betrayed to him at last the secret of her heart.

"I didn't know—I didn't know," Johnny Everard said brokenly. "I didn't know, and oh, my God! I am not worthy of that! I am not worthy of that!"

# CHAPTER XXXIX

## "THE PAYING"

Once again Mr. Philip Slotman was tainting the fragrant sweetness and freshness of the night with the aroma of a large and expensive J.S. Muria.

Once again the big shabby old car stood waiting in the shadows, a quarter of a mile down the road, while he who hired it leaned against the gate under the shadow of the partly ruined barn.

He had not the smallest doubt but that she would come. It was full early yet; but she would come, though, being a woman, she would in all probability be late.

And she would pay, she dared not refuse him. Yet he needed more than the money, he thought, as he leaned at his ease against the gate and smoked his cigar.

And now she was coming. He flung the half-smoked cigar away and waited as the dark figure approached him in the night.

"You are early to-night, Joan." He endeavoured to put softness and tenderness into his voice.

"I am here at the time I appointed."

"To give me my answer—yes, but we won't discuss that now. I want to speak to you about something else."

"Something other than money?"

"Yes, do you think I always put money first?"

"I had thought so, Mr. Slotman."

"You do me a wrong—a great wrong. There is something that I put far ahead of money, of gold. It is you—Joan, listen! you must listen!" He had gripped her arm and held tightly, and as before she did not struggle nor try to win free of him.

"You shall listen to me. I have told you before many times that I love you."

He tried to drag her closer to him. And now she wrenched herself free.

"I came to discuss money with you, not—not impossibilities."

"So—so that is it, is it? I am impossible, am I?"

"To me—utterly. I have only one feeling for you, the deepest scorn. I don't hate you, because you are too mean, too paltry, too low a thing to hate. I have only contempt for you."

He writhed under the cold and cutting scorn of her words and her voice, the evil temper in him worked uppermost.

"So—so that's the talk, is it?" he cried with a foul oath. "That's it, is it? You—you two-penny ha'penny—" He choked foolishly over his words.

"You!" he gasped, "what are you? What have you been? What about you and—"

Again he was silent, writhing with rage.

"Money—yes, it is money-talk, then, and by thunder I'll make you pay! I'll bleed you white, you cursed—" Again more foolish oaths, the clumsy cursing of a man in the grip of passion.

"You shall pay! It's money-talk, yes—you shall pay! We will talk in thousands, my girl. I said five thousand. It isn't enough—what is your good name worth, eh? What is it worth to you? I could paint you a nice colour, couldn't I? What will this fellow Everard say when I tell him what I can tell him? How the village fools will talk it over in their alehouse, eh? And in the cottages, how they will stare at Miss Meredyth of Starden when she takes her walks abroad. They'll wink at one another, won't they. They'll remember! Trust 'em, they'll never forget!"

She felt sickened, faint, and horrified, yet she gave no sign.

"Money you said!" he shouted, "and money it shall be! Ten thousand pounds, or I'll give you away, so that every man and woman in Starden will count 'emselves your betters! I'll give you away to the poor fool you think you are going to marry! There won't be any wedding. I'll swear a man couldn't marry a thing—with such a name as I shall give you! Money, yes! you'll pay! I want ten thousand pounds! Not five, remember, but ten, and perhaps more to follow. And if you don't pay, there won't be many who will not have heard about your imaginary marriage to that dog, Hugh Alston."

The girl drew a deep shuddering sigh. She pressed her hands over her breast. From the shadows about the old barn a deeper shadow moved, something vaulted the gate lightly and came down with a thud on the ground beside Mr. Philip Slotman.

"Joan," said a voice, "you will go away and leave this man to me. I will attend to the paying of him."

Slotman turned, his rage gone, a cold sweat of fear bursting out on his forehead; his loose jaw sagged.

"A—a trap," he gasped.

"To catch a rat! And the rat is caught! Joan, go. I will follow presently."

No word passed between the two men as they watched the girl's figure down the road. She walked slowly; once she seemed to hesitate as though about to turn back. And it was in her mind to turn back, to plead for mercy for this man, this creature. Yet she did not. She flung her head up. No, she would not ask for mercy for him: Hugh Alston was just.

So in silence they watched her till the darkness had swallowed her.

"So you refused to accept my warning, Slotman?"

"I—I refuse to have anything to do with you. It is no business of yours, kindly allow me—"

Slotman would have gone. Hugh thrust out a strong arm and barred his way.

"Wait!" he said, "blackmailer!"

"I—I was asking for a loan."

"A gift of money with threats—lying, infamous threats. How shall I deal with you?" Hugh frowned as in thought. "How can a man deal with a dog like you? Dog—may all dogs forgive me the libel! Shall I thrash you? Shall I tear the clothes from your body, and thrash you and fling you, bleeding and tattered, into that field? Shall I hand you over to the Police?"

"You—you dare not," Slotman said; his teeth were chattering. "It will mean her name being dragged in the mud, the whole thing coming out. You—you dare not do it."

"You are right. I dare not, for the sake of her name—the name of such a woman must never be uttered in connection with such a thing as yourself. How, then, shall I deal with you? It must be the thrashing, yet it is not enough. It is a pity the duel has gone out, not that you would have fought me with a sword or pistol, Slotman, still—Yes, it must be the thrashing."

"If you touch me—"

Hugh laughed sharply. "If I touch you, what?"

"I shall call for help. I shall summon you. I—"

"Put your hands up."

"Help! help! help!"

Down the road the tired chauffeur slumbered peacefully on the seat of the shabby car. He heard nothing, save some distant unintelligible sounds and the cooing of a wood-pigeon in an adjacent thicket.

Henry St. John Cooper

And then presently there came down the road a flying figure, the figure of a man who sobbed as he ran, a man from whom the clothes hung in ribbons, a man with wild staring eyes, and panting, labouring chest. He stumbled as he ran, and picked himself up again, to fall again. So, running, stumbling, falling, he came at last to the car and shrieked at the driver to awaken.

# CHAPTER XL

## "IS IT THE END?"

Lady Linden, wearing a lilac printed cotton sunbonnet, her skirts pinned up about her, was busy with a trowel, disordering certain flower-beds that presently the gardeners would come and put right.

"Idle women," said her ladyship, "are my abomination. How a woman can moon about and do nothing is more than I can understand. Look at me, am I not always busy? From early morning to dewy eve I—Curtis!"

"Yes, my lady?"

"Come here at once," said her ladyship. "I have dug up a worm. I dislike worms. Carry the creature away; don't hurt it, Curtis. I dislike cruelty even to worms. Ugh! How you can touch the thing!"

Curtis, under-gardener, trudged away with a large healthy worm dangling from thumb and forefinger, a sheepish grin on his face.

"Those creatures have none of the finer feelings," thought her ladyship. "Yet we are all brothers and sisters according to

Henry St. John Cooper

the Bible. I don't agree with that at all. Curtis, come back; there is another worm."

Marjorie stood at the window, watching her aunt's operations, yet seeing none of them. Her face was set and white and resolute, the soft round chin seemed to be jutting out more obstinately than usual.

For Marjorie had made up her mind definitely, and she knew that she was about to hurt herself and to hurt someone else.

But it must be. It was only fair, it was only just. Silence, she believed, would be wicked.

The door behind her opened, and Tom Arundel came into the room. He was fresh from the stable, and smelled of straw.

"Why, darling, is there anything up? I got your note asking me to come here at once. Joe gave it to me just as we were going to take out the brute Lady Linden has bought. Of all the vicious beasts! I wish to goodness she wouldn't buy a horse without a proper opinion, but it is useless talking to her. She said she liked the white star on its forehead—white star! black devil, I call it! But I'll break him in if I break my neck—doing it. But—I am sorry. You want me?"

"I want to speak to you."

"Then you might turn and look at a chap, Marjorie."

"I—I prefer to—to look out through the window," she said in a stifled voice.

Standing in the room he beheld her, slim and graceful, dark against the light patch of the window, her back obstinately turned to him; looking at her, there came a great and deep tenderness into his face, the light of a very honest and intense love.

"Tell me, sweetheart, then," he said—"tell me in your own way, what is it? Nothing very serious, is it?" There was a suggestion of laughter in his voice.

"It is very serious, Tom."

"Yes?"

"It—it concerns you—me and you—our future."

"Yes, dear, then it is serious." The laughter was gone; there came a look of fear, of anxiety into his eyes.

It could not be that she was going to discard him, turn him down, end it all now? But she was.

"Tom, it is only right and honest of me to tell you that—that"—her voice shook—"that I have made a mistake."

"That you do not love me?" he said, and his voice was strangely quiet.

"Oh, Tom, I believed I did. It all seemed so different when we used to meet, knowing that everyone was against us. It seemed so romantic, so—so nice, and now ..." Her voice trailed off miserably.

"And now, now, sweet," and his voice was filled with tenderness and yearning, "now I fall far short of what you hoped for."

"Oh, it isn't that. It is I—I—who am to blame, not you. I was a senseless, romantic little fool, a child, and now I am a woman."

"You don't love me, Marjorie?"

Silence for a moment, then she answered in a low voice: "No!"

"Nor ever will, your love can't come back again?"

"I don't think it—it was ever there. I was wrong; I did not understand. I was foolish and weak. I thought it fine to—to steal away and meet you. I think I put a halo of romance about your head, and now—"

"A halo of romance about my head," he repeated. He looked down at his hands, grimed with the work he had been at; he smiled, but there was no mirth in his smile.

This was the end then! And he loved her, Heaven knew how he loved her! He looked at the unyielding little figure against the light, and in his eyes was a great longing and a subdued passion.

"So it—it is the end, Marjorie?"

"I want it to be."

"Yes, I understand. I knew that I was not good enough, never good enough for you—far, far beneath you, dear. Only I would have tried to make you happy—that is what I meant, you understand that? I would have given my life to making you happy, little girl. Perhaps I was a fool to think I could. I know now that I could not."

"Tom, I am sorry," she said. "I am sorry."

He came to her, he put his hand on her arm.

"Don't blame yourself, dear," he said, "don't blame yourself. You can't help your heart; you—you only thought you cared for me for a time, but it was just a fancy, and it—it passed, didn't it? And now it is gone, and can never come back again. Of course it must end. Your wishes—always—mean everything to me." He bent, he touched the white hand with his lips, and then turned away. Once at the door he looked back; but she did not move, the tears were streaming down her cheeks, and she did not want him to see them.

How well he had taken it! How well, and yet he loved her! She realised now how much he loved her, how fine he was, and generous, even Hugh could not have been more generous than he.

And Marjorie stood there like one in a dream, watching, yet seeing nothing, going over in her mind all that had passed, suffering the pain of it. And she had loved him once! Those mystic moonlight meetings, his young arms about her, his lips against hers—oh, she had loved him! And then had come the commonplace, the everyday, sordid side of it, he the accepted lover, high in Lady Linden's favour, which meant the gradual awakening from a dream, her dream of love.

"I am fickle, I am false. I do not know my own mind, and— and I have hurt him. I am not worthy of hurting him. He is better, finer than I ever thought."

Still Lady Linden prodded and trowelled at the neat bed, still she demanded occasional help from the patient Curtis; and now came a man, breathless and coatless, rushing across the lawn. He had news for her, something that must be told; gone was his accustomed terror of her ladyship. He told her what he had to say, and she dropped the trowel and ran— actually ran as Marjorie had never seen her run.

She could have laughed, but for the pain at her heart. He had taken it so well; he had risen to a height she had not suspected him capable of, and the fault was hers, hers.

What was that? What were they carrying? God help her I What was that they were carrying across the lawn? Why did they walk so quietly, so carefully? Why ask?

She knew! Instinct told her. She knew! She flung out her hands and gripped at the window-frame and watched. She saw her aunt, her usually ruddy face drawn, haggard, and white. She saw something that lay motionless on a part of the old barn-door, which four men were carrying with such care. She saw a man on a bicycle dashing off down the drive.

Why ask? She knew! And only just now, a few short minutes ago—no, no, a lifetime ago—she had told him she did not love him.

"An accident, Marjorie." Lady Linden's voice was harsh, unlike her usual round tones. "An accident—that brute of a horse—girl, don't, don't faint."

"I am not going to. I want to help—him."

They had brought Tom Arundel into the house, had laid him on a bed in an upper room. The village doctor had come, and, finding something here beyond his skill, had sent off, with Lady Linden's full approval, an urgent message to a surgeon of repute, and now they were waiting—waiting the issues of life and death.

The servants looked at the white-faced, distraught girl pityingly. They remembered that she was to have been the dying man's wife. The whole thing had been so sudden, was so shocking and tragic. No wonder that she looked like death herself; they could not guess at the self-reproach, the self-denunciation, nor could Lady Linden.

"No one," said her ladyship, "is to blame but me. It was my doing, my own pig-headed folly. The boy told me that the horse was a brute, and I—I said that he—if he hadn't the pluck to try and break him in—I would find someone who would. I am his murderess!" her ladyship cried tragically. "Yes, Marjorie, look at me—look at the murderess of the man you love!"

"Aunt!"

"It is true. Revile me! I alone am guilty. I've robbed you of your lover." Lady Linden was nearer to hysterics at this moment than ever in her life.

"How long? how long?" she demanded impatiently. "How long will it be before that fool comes?"

The fool was the celebrated surgeon wired for to London. He had wired back that he was on his way; no man could do more.

But the waiting, the horrible waiting; the ceaseless watching and listening for the sound of wheels, the strange hush that had fallen upon the house, the knowledge that there in an upper chamber death was waiting, waiting to take a young life.

Hours, every minute of which had seemed like hours themselves, hours had passed. Lady Linden sat with her hands clenched and her eyes fixed on nothingness. She blamed herself with all her honest hearty nature; she blamed herself even more unsparingly than in the past she had blamed others for their trifling faults.

Henry St. John Cooper

Her self-recriminations had got on Marjorie's nerves. She could not bear to sit here and listen to her aunt when all the time she knew that it was she—she alone who was to blame. She had told him that she did not love him, that all his hopes must end, that the future they had planned between them should never be, and so had sent him to his death.

She waited outside in the big hall, her eyes on the stairs, her ears tensioned to every sound from above, and at every sound she started.

Voices at last, low and muffled, voices pitched in a low key, men talking as in deep confidence. She heard and she watched. She saw the two men, the doctor and the surgeon, descending the stairs; she rose and went to meet them, yet said never a word.

She watched their faces; she saw that they looked grave. She saw that the face of the great man was worn and tired. She looked in vain for something that would whisper the word "Hope" to her.

"Miss Linden is engaged to Mr. Arundel," the local doctor said.

The great man held out his hand to her. He knew so well, how many thousands of times had he seen, that same look of questioning, pitiful in its dumbness.

He held her hand closely, "There is hope. That is all I care say to you—just a hope, and that is all."

It was all that he dared to say, the utmost to which he could go. He knew that false hopes, raised only to be crushed, were cruelty. And he had never done that, never would. "There is yet one ray of hope. He may live; I can say no more than that, Miss Linden."

And, little though it was, it was almost more than she had dared to hope for.

# CHAPTER XLI

## MR. RUNDLE TAKES A HAND

Battered and sorely bruised, Philip Slotman lay on his bed in the Feathers Inn in Little Langbourne, and cursed his luck. Every time he moved he swore to himself.

He was hurt in mind, body, and estate; he was consumed by a great rage and a sense of injury. He had suffered, and someone should pay—Joan mainly, after Joan, Hugh Alston. But it would be safer to make Joan pay. Not in money. Alston had insisted on it that he had nothing to expect in the way of cash from Miss Meredyth.

Slotman lay writhing, and cursing and planning vengeance. There were few things that he would not have liked to do to Hugh Alston, but finally he decided he could better hurt Hugh Alston through Joan, so thereafter he devoted his thoughts to Joan.

The church bells of Little Langbourne Church were ringing pleasantly when Philip Slotman, with many a grunt and inward groan, rose from his couch.

Except for a slight discoloration about the left eye and a certain stiffness of gait, there was nothing about Philip

Slotman when he came down to the coffee-room for his breakfast to suggest that he had seen so much trouble the previous evening. But there were some who had seen Slotman come in, and among them was the waiter. He put his hand over his mouth, and smirked now at the sight of Slotman, and Slotman noticed it.

The bells rang no message of peace and good-will to Mr. Slotman this morning.

Yes, Joan would be the one. He would make her pay; he would hurt Alston through her, and hit her hard at the same time. He would stay here at Little Langbourne.

"Buddesby, sir?" said the waiter. "Yes, sir. Mister John Everard's place about a quarter of a mile beyond the village. Very interesting old 'ouse, sir, one of the best farms hereabouts. Mr. Everard's a well-to-do gentleman, sir, old family, not—"

"Oh, go away!"

The waiter withdrew. "Anyhow," he thought, "he got it all right last night, and serve him right. Law! what a mess 'e were in when he came in."

A quarter of a mile beyond the village. Slotman nodded. He would go. He remembered that Alston had said something last night about this man Everard, had suggested all sorts of things might happen to him, Slotman, if he communicated in any way with Everard.

"Anyhow I shall tell him, and unless he is a born fool he will soon get quit of her. By thunder! I'll make her name reek, as I told her I would. I'll set this place and Starden and half the infernal country talking about her! If she shews her face anywhere, she'll get stared at. I'll let her and that beast Alston see what it means to get on the wrong side of a chap like me."

A quarter of a mile beyond the village. Thank Heaven it was no further.

The church bells had ceased ringing, from the church itself came the pleasant sounds of voices. The village street lay white in the sunlight with the blue shadows of the houses, a world of peace and of beauty, of sweet scenes and of sweet sounds; and now he had left the village behind him.

"Is this Buddesby, my man? Those gates, are they the gates of Buddesby?"

"Aye, they be," said the man. He was a big, gipsy-looking fellow, who slouched with hunched shoulders and a yellow mongrel dog at his heels.

"The gates of Buddesby they be, and—" He paused; he stared hard into Slotman's face.

"Oh!" he said slowly, "oh, so 'tis 'ee, be it? I been watching out for 'ee."

"What—what do you mean?"

"I remember 'ee, I do. I remember your grinning face. I've carried it in my memory all right. See that dawg?" The man pointed to the lurcher. "See him: he's more'n a brother, more'n a son, more'n a wife to me. That's the dawg you run over that day, and you grinned. I seen it—you grinned!" The man's black eyes sparkled. He looked swiftly up the road and down it, and Slotman saw the action and quivered.

"I'll give you—" he began. "I am very sorry; it was an accident. I'll pay you for—"

But the man with the blazing eyes had leaped at him.

"I been waiting for 'ee, and I've cotched 'ee at last!" he shouted.

\*　\*　\*　\*　\*

Johnny Everard, hands in pockets, mooning about his stock and rickyard, this calm Sunday morning, never guessed how near he had been to receiving a visitor.

He had not seen Joan since that night when, with Ellice beside him, he had seen her and the man at the door of Mrs. Bonner's cottage.

He had meant to go, but had not gone. He was due there to-day; this very morning Helen would expect him. He had never missed spending a Sunday with them since the engagement; and yet he felt loath to go, and did not know why.

He had seen Connie off to Church. Con never missed. Ellice had not gone. Ellice was perhaps a little less constant than Con. He wondered where the girl was now, and, thinking of her, the frown on his face was smoothed away.

Always there was wonder, a sense of unreality in his mind; a feeling that somehow, in some way, he was wrong. He must be wrong. Strangely enough, these last few days he had thought more constantly of Ellice than of Joan. He had pictured her again and again to himself—a little, white-clad, barefooted figure standing against the dusky background of the hallway, framed by the open door. He remembered the colour in her cheeks, and her brave championship of the other woman; but he remembered most of all the look in her eyes when she had said to him, "Please, please don't!"

"I shall never kiss her again," he said, and said it to himself, and knew as he said it that he was denying himself the thing for which now he longed.

He had kissed Joan's cold cheek, he had kissed her hand, but her lips had not been for him. He had wondered once if they ever would be, and he had cared a great deal; now he ceased to wonder.

"I shall never kiss Gipsy again," he thought, and, turning, saw her.

"So you—you didn't go to Church, Gipsy?"

"I thought you had gone to Starden."

They stood and looked at one another.

"No. I don't think I shall go to Starden to-day."

"But they expect you."

"I—I don't think I shall go to-day, Gipsy. Shall we go for a walk across the fields?"

"You ought to go to Starden," she said. "She—she will expect you."

But a spirit of reckless defiance had come to him.

"She won't miss me if I don't go."

"No, she won't miss you," the girl said softly, and her

voice shook.

"So—so come with me, Gipsy girl."

"If you wish it."

"You know I do."

Yet when they went together across the fields, when they came to the edge of the hop-garden and saw the neatly trailing vines, which this year looked better and more promising than he could ever remember before, they had nothing to say to one another, not a word. Once he took her hand and held it for a moment, then let it go again; and at the touch of her he thrilled, little dreaming how her heart responded.

He scarcely looked at her. If he had, he might have seen a glow in her cheeks, a brightness in her eyes, the brightness born of a new and wonderful hope.

"After all, after all," the girl was thinking. "I believe he cares for me a little—not so much as he loves her, but a little, a little, and I love him."

Connie smiled on them as they came in together. It was as she liked to see them. She noticed the deep colouring in the girl's cheeks, the new brightness in her eyes, and Connie, who always acted on generous impulses, kissed her.

"What's that for?" Johnny cried. "Haven't you one for me too, Con?"

"Always, always," she said. She put her arms about his neck and hugged him.

It seemed as if the clouds that had so long overcast this little house had drifted away this calm Sabbath day, and the sun was shining down gloriously on them.

For some time Connie had been quietly watching the girl. There came back into her memory a promise given long ago. "I will do nothing, nothing, Con, unless I tell you first."

She knew Ellice for the soul of honour; she had felt safe, and now she was waiting.

"Well, Ellice, have you anything to say to me?" Johnny was gone after dinner to his tiny study to wrestle with letters and figures that he abhorred.

"Yes," Ellice said.

"I thought you had—well?"

"I am going to Starden," the girl said. "I am going to Starden this afternoon, Con."

"What for?"

"To see—her?"

"Why—why, darling, why?"

"To ask her if she can be generous—and oh, I believe she can—to ask her why she is taking him away from me when I love him so, and when—oh, Con—Con, when I believe that he cares a little for me."

Con held out her arms, she caught the girl tightly.

"My love and my prayers and my wishes will go with you, darling."

# CHAPTER XLII

## "WALLS WE CANNOT BATTER DOWN"

"Why?" Helen asked. "Why isn't Johnny here to-day, Joan?"

"I do not know," Joan said. She had scarcely given a thought to Johnny Everard that morning. All her thoughts had been of two men, the men she had left in the darkness by the roadside. She blamed herself bitterly now that she had left them; she trembled to think what might have happened.

"Helen, if Johnny Everard does come, I wish to speak to him. I have a good deal to say to him. I want to be alone with him for some time."

"Of course, darling." But there was anxious enquiry in Helen's face.

Surely, surely there had been no quarrel between them? Johnny was not one to quarrel with anyone, yet it was strange that he had not been here for so many days, and that this being Sunday still he was not here.

"When he comes," Joan was thinking, "I shall tell him— everything." She knew she would hate it; she knew that she would feel that in some way she was lowering herself. It

Henry St. John Cooper

would be a horrible confession for one with her stubborn pride to have to make. Not of guilt and wrongdoing, but that such should be ascribed to her.

Helen was watching from the window, her mind filled with worries and doubts.

A man had turned in by the gates, was walking slowly up the winding drive.

It was Johnny, of course. Helen saw it all. The car had gone wrong, but Johnny, not to miss this Sunday, had walked.

"Joan, Johnny is coming," she called out. "He is walking. He—" She paused; it was not Johnny. She was silent; she stared for a moment. The man looked familiar, then she knew who it was.

"Joan, it is Mr. Alston," she said quietly. "What does he want here?" And Helen's voice was filled with suspicion.

"Thank Heaven," Joan thought, "thank Heaven that he is here."

For the first time Hugh Alston knocked for admission on the Starden door. A score of times he had asked himself, "Shall I go?" And he could find no answer. He had come at last.

"What can he want? I did not know he was here in Starden. I didn't even know that he knew where Joan was. I don't understand this business at all," Helen was thinking.

A servant shewed him in. Joan shook hands with him. Helen did so, under an air of graciousness which hid a cold hostility. What was this man doing here? If he was nothing to Joan, and Joan was nothing to him, why did he come?

And how could he be anything to Joan when she was to marry Johnny?

So this was her home! A fit setting for her loveliness, and yet he knew of a fitter, of another home where she could shine to even greater advantage. They talked of commonplace things, hiding their feelings behind words, waiting, Joan and Hugh, till Helen should leave them. But Helen lingered with less than her usual tact, lingered with a mind filled with vague suspicions, wondering why Johnny had not come.

Sitting near the window she could see the drive, and presently a young girl on an old bicycle coming up it. Helen stared.

"Why, here is Ellice Brand," she said, and fears took possession of her. There was something wrong! Johnny was ill, or had met with an accident. Ellice had ridden over to tell them.

"I'll go and see her, Joan," she said, and so at last was gone.

Hugh closed the door after her.

"You've been anxious?" he said briefly.

"Naturally!"

"There was no need. I had to give him what I had promised him, one must always keep one's word. It was rather a brutal business, Joan, but I had to go through with it. I'd sooner not tell you anything more. I am not proud of it."

"I—I understand, and you can understand that I was anxious."

"For him?"

"For—for you."

"For me?" He took two long strides to her. "Joan, are you going to let your pride rear impassable walls between us for ever? Can't you be fair, generous, natural, true to yourself? Can't you see how great, how overwhelming my love for you is?"

"There is—is something more than pride between us, Hugh."

"There is nothing—nothing that cannot be broken; that cannot be forced and broken down," he said eagerly. "You are to marry a man you do not love. Why should you? Would it be fair to yourself? Would it be fair to me? Would it be fair to your future? Think while there is time."

"I cannot," she said. "I have given him my promise—and I shall stand by it." She drew her hands away. "It is useless, Hugh. Useless now—if I did rear walls of pride between you and myself. I confess it now, I did; but they are so strong that we may not break them down."

"They shall be broken down!" he said. "Answer me this—this question truthfully, and from your soul. Look into my eyes, and answer me in one word, yes or no?" He held her hands again; he held her so that she must face him, and so holding her, looking into her eyes, he asked her: "Do you love me? Have you given to me some of your heart, knowing that I have given all of mine to you, knowing that I love you so, and need you and long for you? Do you love me a little in return, Joan?"

She was silent; her eyes met his bravely enough, yet it seemed as if she had no control upon her lips, the word would not come. Once before she had lied to him, and knew that she could not lie again, not with his eyes looking deep into hers, probing the very secrets of her soul.

"Joan, do you love me? My Joan, do you love me?" And then the answer came at last—"Yes."

Henry St. John Cooper

# CHAPTER XLIII

## "NOT TILL THEN WILL I GIVE UP HOPE"

"There is nothing wrong, nothing the matter with Johnny or Connie?"

"Nothing."

"Then why—why did not Johnny come?"

"He is busy."

"But you—"

"I came to see Joan Meredyth," said Ellice quietly. She and Helen did not like one another; they were both frank in their dislike. Helen looked down on Ellice as a person of no importance, who was entirely unwanted, a mere nuisance, someone for ever in the way.

Ellice looked on Helen as the promoter of this engagement and marriage, as the woman who was responsible for everything. She did not like her. She resented her; but for Helen, there would never have been any break in the old happy life at Buddesby.

"So you wish to see Joan, why?"

"Privately."

"My dear child, surely—"

"I am not a child, and I wish to see Joan Meredyth privately, and surely I have the right, Mrs. Everard?"

Helen frowned. "Well, at any rate you cannot see her now. She is engaged, a friend is with her."

"I can wait."

"Very well," Helen said. "If you insist. Does Johnny know that you are here?" she asked with sudden suspicion.

"No; Connie knows. I told her, and I am willing to wait."

Helen looked at her. Helen was honest. "I thought the child pretty," she reflected, "and I was wrong; she is beautiful. I don't understand it. In some extraordinary way she seems to have changed." But her manner towards Ellice was as unfriendly as before.

"I do not in the least know how long Joan will be. You may have to wait a considerable time."

"I shall not mind."

In the room these two stood, Joan had made her confession frankly, truthfully. She had admitted her love for him, but of hope for the future she had none. That she loved him now, in spite of all the past, in spite of the troubles and shame he had brought on her, was something that had happened in spite of herself, against her will, against her desire; but because it was so, she admitted it frankly.

"But my love for you, Hugh, matters nothing," she said. "Because I love you I shall suffer more—but I shall never break my word to the man I have given it to."

"When you stand before the altar with that man's ring on your finger, when you have promised before God to be his wife, then and not till then will I give up hope. And that will be never. It is your pride, dear, your pride that ever fights against your happiness and mine; but I shall beat it down and humble it, Joan, and win you in the end. Your own true, sweet self."

"I don't think I have any pride left," she said. "I was prouder when I was poor than I am now. My pride was then all I had; it kept me above the sordid life about me. I cultivated it, I was glad of it, but since then—Oh, Hugh, I am not proud any more, only very humble, and very unhappy."

And because she was still promised to another man, he could not, as he would, hold out his arms to her and take her to his breast and comfort her. Instead, he took her hand and held it tightly for a time, then lifted it to his lips and went, leaving her; yet went with a full hope for the future in his heart, for he had wrung from her the confession that she loved him.

In the hall a girl, sitting there waiting patiently, looked at him with great dark eyes, yet he never saw her. A servant let him out, and then the servant came back to her. "Tell Miss Meredyth that I am here waiting to see her," Ellice said.

And as the man went away she wondered what had brought Hugh Alston here to-day, why he should be here so long with Joan when she could so distinctly remember Joan's lack of recognition of him in the village. She could also remember the sight of them that night, their dark shapes against the yellow glow of the lamplight in Mrs. Bonner's cottage.

How would she find Joan? she wondered. Softened, perhaps even confused, some of her coldness shaken, some of her self-possession gone? But no, Joan held out a hand in greeting to her.

"I did not know that you were here, Miss Brand," she said. "Have you not seen Mrs. Everard?"

"I have seen her," Ellice said, "but I didn't come here to-day to see her. I came to see you."

"To see me?" Joan smiled—a conventional smile. "You will sit down, won't you? Is it anything that I can do? It is not, I hope, that Mr. Everard is ill?"

"And—and if he were," the girl cried, "would you care?"

Joan started, her face grew colder.

"I do not understand."

"Yes, you—you do. Why are you marrying him? Why are you taking him from me when—"

"Taking him from—you?" Joan's voice was like ice water on flames of fire. Ellice was silent.

"Miss Meredyth, I came here to-day to see you, to speak to you, to—to open my heart to you." Her lips trembled. "Perhaps I am wrong, perhaps I have no right to be here to say what I am going to say. I told Connie; she—she knows that I have come here, and she knows why."

"Yes; go on."

"If—if you loved him it would be different. I would not dare think of saying anything then. I think I would be glad. I could, at any rate, be reconciled to it, because it would be for his happiness. If you loved him—but you don't—you don't! He is a man who could not live without love. It is part of his life. He might think, might believe that he would be content to take you because you are lovely and—and good and clever, and all those things that I am not, even though you do not love him, but the time would come when his heart would ache for the love you withheld. Oh, Joan—Joan, forgive me—forgive me, but I must speak. I think you would if you were in my place!"

The cold bitterness was passing slowly from Joan's face. There came a tinge of colour into her cheeks; her eyes that watched the girl grew softer and more tender.

"Go on," she said; "go on, tell me!"

"I have nothing more to say."

"Yes, you have—you have much more. You have this to say—you love him and want him, you wish to take him from me. Is that it, Ellice?"

"If you loved him I would not have dared to come. I would have told myself that I was content. But you don't. I have watched you—yes, spied on you—looking for some sign of tenderness that would prove to me that you loved him; but it never came. And so I know that you are marrying Johnny Everard with no love, accepting all the great love that he is offering to you and giving him nothing in exchange. Oh, it is not fair!"

"It is not fair," Joan said; "it is not fair, and yet I thought of that. I told him just what you have told me, and still he seemed to be content."

"Because he loves you so, and because he has hope in the future, because in spite of everything he still hopes that he might win your heart, and I know that he never can."

"How do you know that?"

"Because I—I think you have already given your heart away."

And now Joan's eyes flamed, the anger came back. "By what right do you say that? How dared you say that?"

"It is only what I believed. I believed that a woman so sweet, so beautiful, so good as you, must love. You could not live your life without love. If it has not come yet, then it will come some day, and then if you are his—his wife, it will come too late. You are made for love, Joan, just as he is. You could not live your life without it—you would feel need for it. Oh yes, you think I am a child, a foolish, romantic schoolgirl, a stupid little thing, talking, talking, but in your heart you know that I am right."

"But if he—loves me," Joan said softly, "if he loves me, little Ellice, then how can I break my word to him?"

"I do not ask you to break your word to him, only tell him, tell him the truth again. Tell him what I have told you, tell him—if there is someone else, if you have already met someone you care for—tell him that too, so that he will know how impossible it must ever be that you will give him the love he hoped to win. Tell him that, be frank and truthful. Remember, it is for all your lives—all his life and all yours.

When he realises that your heart can never be his, do you think he will not surfer more, will not his sufferings be longer drawn out than if you told him so frankly now? If the break was to come now, to come and be ended for ever—but to live together, to live a mock life, to live beneath the same roof, to share one another's lives, and yet know one another's souls to be miles and miles apart—oh, Joan, you would suffer, and he too, he perhaps even more than you."

"And you love him?" Joan said softly. "You love him, Ellice?"

"With all my heart and soul. I would die for him. It—it sounds foolish, this sort of thing is foolish, the kind of words a silly girl would say, yet it is the truth."

"I think it is," Joan said. "But then, dear, if he loves me, he could not love you?"

"I think he might," Ellice said softly.

She was thinking of the morning, of the look she had seen in his eyes, the awakening look of a man who sees things he has been blind to.

"I think he might," her heart echoed. "I think he might, in time, in a little time." And did not know, could not guess, that even at this moment Johnny Everard, sitting alone in his little study with untended papers strewn about him, was thinking of her—thinking of the look he had seen in her eyes that very day, out in the sunshine of the fields.

"So you came to me to tell me. It was brave of you?"

"I had to come. I could not have come if you had been different from what you are."

"Then, even though I am taking away the man you love from you, you do not hate me?"

"Hate you? Sometimes I think I wished I could—but I could not. If I had hated you, if I had thought you cold and hard to all the world, I would not be here. I have come to plead to you because you are generous and honest, true and good. I could not have come otherwise."

"What must I do, little Ellice?"

"Tell him the truth, if there is—"

"There is—yet that could never come to anything."

"Why not?"

"Because—ah, you can't understand."

"Still, your heart is not your own; you could never give it to Johnny Everard."

"And I must tell him so, and then—"

"And then you will ask him if he would be content to live all his life without love, knowing that he will never, never win your heart, because it would be impossible."

"But I have given him my promise, Ellice."

"I know, I know; and you will not break it, because you could not break a promise. But you will tell him this, and offer him his freedom; it will be for him to decide."

Joan stood for many moments in silence, her hand still resting on the girl's shoulder. Then she drew Ellice to her;

she thrust back the shining hair, and kissed the girl's forehead. "I think—yes, I think I shall do all this, Ellice," she said.

# CHAPTER XLIV

## POISON

"Johnny! Johnny! Have you gone to sleep, dear? There is someone here to see you."

"Eh?" Johnny started into wakefulness, he huddled his untidy papers together. "I must have been dozing off. I was thinking. Con, is Gipsy back yet?"

"Not yet, and I am getting a little anxious about her; it is almost dusk. But there is someone here asking for you."

"Who?"

"A man, a—a—gentleman, I suppose. He looks as if he has been drinking, though."

"A nice sort of visitor for a Sunday evening. What is his name, Con?"

"Slotman."

"Don't know it. I suppose I'd better see him. Wait, I'll light the lamp. If Ellice isn't back soon I shall go and hunt for her. Do you know which direction she went in?"

"I—I think—" Connie hesitated; she was never any good at concealment. "I think she went towards Starden."

"Then when we've got rid of this fellow I'll get out the car and go and find her. Show him in, Con."

Mr. Philip Slotman, looking shaken, bearing on his face several patches of court plaster, which were visible, and in his breast a black fury that was invisible, came in.

"Mr. Slotman?"

"Yes, you are Mr. Everard?"

Johnny nodded pleasantly. "If it is business, Sunday evening is hardly the time—"

"It is personal and private business, Mr. Everard."

The man, Johnny decided, was not, as Con had supposed, drunk, but he had evidently been in the wars. It was surprising the number of places in which he seemed to be wounded. He walked stiffly, he carried his right arm stiffly. His face was decorated with plaster, and his obviously very good clothes were torn; for what Hugh Alston had commenced so ably last night, Rundle had completed this morning.

"It is private and personal, my business with you. I understand you are engaged to be married to a lady in whom I have felt some interest."

Johnny looked up and stiffened.

"Well?"

"I allude to Miss Joan Meredyth, for some time engaged by

me as a typist in my city office."

"Well?"

"Miss Meredyth did not always hold the position in society that she does now."

"I am aware of that."

"There may be a great deal that you are not aware of," said Slotman; and Slotman was quivering with rage at the indignities he had been subjected to.

"You will forgive me," said Johnny, "but I do not propose to discuss my future wife with a stranger—with anyone at all, in fact, and certainly not with a stranger."

"And you will forgive me," said Slotman, "but when you have heard what I have to say, I very much doubt if you will regard Miss Joan Meredyth in the light of your future wife."

Johnny moved towards the door and opened it.

"I think it will be better if you go," he said quietly.

"If you do, you will be sorry when it is too late. I come here as a friend—"

"You will go!"

"In June, nineteen hundred and eighteen, when Joan Meredyth was a girl at school—"

"I have told you that I will not listen."

"She gave it out that she was leaving England for Australia.

She never went in reality, she—

"Once more I order you to go before I—"

"In reality she was living with Mr. Hugh Alston as his wife—"

Philip Slotman laughed nervously.

"Liar!"

"I had to tell you in spite of yourself, and it is true. It is true. Ask Lady Linden of Cornbridge; she knows. She believes to this day that Joan Meredyth and Alston were married, and they never were. I have searched the registers at Marlbury and—"

"Will you go? You seem to have been hurt. You have probably carried this lying story elsewhere and have received what you merited. I hardly like to touch you now, but unless you go—"

"I am going." Slotman moved stiffly towards the door. "Ask Lady Linden of Cornbridge. She believes to this day that Joan Meredyth is Hugh Alston's wife."

"By heavens! If you don't go—"

Slotman glanced at him; he saw that he was over-stepping the danger-line. Yes, he must go, and quickly, so he went. But he had planted the venom; he had left it behind him. He had forced this man to hear, even though he would not listen.

"First blow," Slotman thought, "the first blow at her! And I ain't done yet! no, I ain't done yet. I'll make her writhe—"

He paused. He had not carried out his intention in full, this man had not given him time. Of course, if it was only Joan's money that this fellow Everard was after, the story would make little or no difference. The marriage would go on all the same, if it was a matter of money, but—

Philip Slotman retraced his painful steps. Once again he tapped on the door of Buddesby.

"There was something that I wished to say to Mr. Everard that I entirely forgot—a small matter," he said to the servant. "Don't trouble, I know the way."

He pushed past the girl into the house. Johnny, staring before him into vacancy, trying to realise this incredible, impossible thing that the man had told him, started. He looked up. In the doorway stood Mr. Slotman.

"By Heaven!" said Johnny, and sprang up. "If you don't go—"

"Wait! You don't think I should be such a fool as to come to you with a lying story, a story that could not be substantiated? What I have told you is the truth. You may not believe it, because you don't want to. You are marrying a young lady with ample possessions; that may weigh with you. Now, rightly or wrongly, I hold that Miss Meredyth owes me a certain sum of money. I want that money. It doesn't matter to me whether I get it from her or from you. If you like to pay her debt, I will guarantee silence. I shall carry this true story no further if you will undertake to pay me immediately following your marriage with her the sum of ten thousand—"

In spite of his stiffness and his sores, Mr. Slotman turned; he fled, he ran blindly down the hall, undid the hall door, and let himself out, and then without a glance behind, he fled across the wide garden till he reached the road, panting and shaking. And now for the first time he looked back, and as he did so a blinding white glare seemed to strike his eyes; he staggered, and tried to spring aside. Then something struck him, and the black world about him seemed to vomit tongues of red and yellow flame.

The occupants of the fast-travelling touring car felt the horrible jolt the car gave. A woman shrieked. The chauffeur shouted an oath born of fear and horror as he applied his brakes. He stood up, yet for a moment scarcely dared to look back. The woman in the car was moaning with the shock of it; and when he looked he saw something lying motionless, a dark patch against the dim light on the road.

# CHAPTER XLV

## THE GUIDING HAND

Tom Arundel opened his eyes to the sunshine. He had left behind him a world of darkness and of pain, a curiously jumbled unreal world, in which it seemed to him that he had played the part of a thing that was being dragged by unseen hands in a direction that he knew he must not go, a direction against which he fought with all his strength. And yet, in spite of all his efforts, he knew himself to be slipping, slowly but surely slipping.

Then out of the blackness and chaos grew something real and tangible, a pair of small white hands, and on the finger of one of these hands was a ring that he remembered well, for it was a ring that he himself had placed on that finger, and the hands were held out to him, and he clutched at them.

Yet still the fight was not over, still the unseen force dragged and tugged at him, yet he knew that he was winning, because of the little white hands that yet possessed such wonderful strength.

And now he lay, wide-eyed in the sunshine, and the blackness and chaos were gone, but he could still see the hands, for one of them was clasped in his own, and lifting his eyes

304          Henry St. John Cooper

he saw the face that he knew must be there—a pale face, thinner than when he had seen it last, a face that had lost some of its childish prettiness. Yet the eyes had lost nothing, but had gained much. There was tenderness and pity and joy too in them.

"Marjorie," he said, and the weakness of his own voice surprised him, and he lay wondering if it were he who had spoken. "Thank you," he said. He was thanking her for the help those little hands had given him, yet she was not to know that. So for a long time he lay, his breath gentle and regular, the small hand clasped in his own. And now he was away in dreams, not the black and terrifying dreams of just now, but dreams of peace and of a happiness that might never be. And in those dreams she whom he loved bent over him and kissed him on the lips, and said something to him that set the thin blood leaping in his veins.

Tom Arundel opened his eyes again, and knew that it had been no dream. Her lips were still on his; her face, rosy now, almost as of old, was touching his.

"Marjorie," he whispered, "you told me—"

"I told you what was not true, but I thought it was—oh, I believed it was, dear. I believed it was the truth—but I knew afterwards it was not."

"I—I got hurt, didn't I? I can't remember—I remember but dimly—a horse, Marjorie. You don't think—you don't think I did that on purpose after what you said?"

"No, no!" she said. "I know better. Perhaps I did think it, but oh, Tom, I was not worth it! I was not worth it!"

"You are worth all the world to me," he said, "all the world and more."

Lady Linden opened the door. She came in, treading softly; she came to the bedside and looked at him and then at the girl.

"You were talking. I heard your voice. Was he conscious?"

"Yes."

"Thank God!" Lady Linden looked at the girl severely. "I suppose you will be the next invalid—women of your type always overdo it. How many nights is it since you had your clothes off?"

"That does not matter now."

"By rights you should go to bed at once."

"Aunt, I shall not leave him."

Lady Linden sniffed. "Very well; I can do nothing with you."

"Defiant!" she thought to herself. "She is getting character, that girl, after all, and about time. Well, it doesn't matter, now that Tom will live."

Lady Linden went downstairs. "Obstinate and defiant, new role—very well, I am content. She is developing character, and that is a great thing."

He was going to live. It was more than hope now, it was certainty, after days, even weeks of anxiety, of watching and waiting; and this bright morning Lady Linden felt and looked ten years younger as she stepped out into the garden to bully her hirelings.

Jordan, her ladyship's coachman, was sunning himself at the stable door. He took his pipe out hurriedly and hid it behind his back.

"Jordan," said Lady Linden, "you are an old man."

"Not so wonderful old, my lady."

"You have lived all your life with horses."

"With 'osses mainly, my lady."

"How long would it take you, Jordan, to learn to drive a motor car?"

"Me?" He gasped at her in sheer astonishment.

"Jordan, we are both old, but we must move with the times. Horses are dangerous brutes. I have taken a dislike to them. I shall never sit behind another unless it is in a hearse—and then I shan't sit. Jordan, you shall learn to drive a car."

"Shall I?" thought Jordan as her ladyship turned away. "We'll see about that."

Again Tom opened his eyes, and he saw that face above him, and even as he looked the head was bent lower and lower till once again the red lips touched his own.

"Marjorie, is it only pity?" he whispered.

But she shook her head. "It is love, all my love—I know now. It is all ended. I know the truth. Oh, Tom, it—it was you all the time, and after all it was only you!"

# CHAPTER XLVI

## "—SHE HAS GIVEN!"

Never so slowly as to-day had John Everard driven the six and a half miles that divided Buddesby and Little Langbourne from Starden. Never had his frank and open and cheerful face been so clouded and overcast. Many worries, many doubts and fears and uncertainties, were at work in John Everard's mind.

No doubts and uncertainties of anyone but of himself. It was himself—his own feelings, his own belief in himself, his own belief in his love that he was doubting. So he drove very slowly the six and a half miles to Starden, because he had many questions to ask of himself, questions to which answers did not come readily.

"Gipsy is right, she always is," he thought. "She is finer-minded, better, more generous than I am. Her mind could not harbour one doubt of anyone she loved, and I—" He frowned.

Helen Everard, from an upper window, saw his arrival, and watching him as he drove up the approach to the house, marked the frown on his brow, the lack of his usual cheerfulness.

Henry St. John Cooper

"There is something wrong; there seems to be nothing, but something wrong all the time," she thought with a sigh.

"If, after all the trouble I have taken, my plans should come to nothing, I shall be bitterly disappointed. I blame Connie. Con's unworldliness is simply silly. Oh, these people!"

"It is a long time since I saw you, Johnny—four or five days, isn't it?" Joan said. She held out her hand to him, and he took it. He seemed to hesitate, and then drew a little closer and kissed her cheek.

Something wrong. She too saw it, but it did not disturb her as it did Helen.

"Yes, four days—five—I forget," he said, scarcely realising what an admission was this from him, who awhile ago had counted every hour jealously that had kept them apart.

For a few minutes they talked of indifferent things, each knowing it for a preliminary of something to follow.

He had come to tell her something, Joan felt.

"She has something to say to me," Johnny knew. So for a few minutes they fenced, and then it was he who broke away.

He rose, and began to move about the room, as a man disturbed in his mind usually does. She sat calm and expectant, watching him, a faint smile on her lips, a kindness and a gentleness in her face that made it inexpressibly sweet.

"I think, Johnny, you have something to say to me."

"Something that I hate saying. Joan, last night a man—a man

I have never seen before—came to see me."

She stiffened. The faint smile was gone; her face had become as a mask, hard and cold, icy.

"Yes?"

"A man who had something to tell me—you will do me the justice to believe that I did not wish to hear him, that I tried to silence him, but he would not be silenced. He told me lies! foul lies about you! lies!" Johnny said passionately, "things which I, knowing you, know to be untrue. Yet he told them. I drove him out of the place. Then he came back. He had remembered what his errand was—blackmail. He came to me for money. But—but he did not stay, and then—" Johnny paused. He had reached the window, and stood staring out into the garden, yet seeing nothing of its beauty.

"You know," he went on, "that I do not ask you nor expect you to deny—there is no need. What he said I know to be untrue. The man was a villain, one of the lowest, but he has been paid."

"Paid?" she said. She stared.

"Not in money," Johnny said shortly, "in another way."

"You—you struck him?"

"No. I would have; but he saw the danger and fled from it—fled from the punishment that I would have meted out to him to a harder that Fate had in store for him."

"I don't understand."

"Just outside my gate he was knocked down by a car and

very badly injured; it is hardly probable that he will live. The people who knocked him down came hammering on my door. We got him to the Cottage Hospital. In spite of everything I felt sorry for the poor wretch—but that has nothing to do with it now. I came to tell you what happened."

"And yet do not ask me to explain?"

"Of course not!" He swung round and faced her for a moment. "Do you think I would put that indignity on you, Joan?"

"You are very generous, Johnny—why?"

She waited, listening expectantly for his answer. It was some time in coming.

"I am not generous. I simply know that for you to be other than honourable and innocent, pure and good, would be an impossibility."

"Why do you know that?"

"Because I know you."

She smiled. The answer she had almost dreaded to hear had not come. Yet it should have been so simple, so ample an answer to her question. Had he said, "Because I love you," it would have been enough; but he had said, "Because I know you"; and so she smiled.

"Johnny, I have something to say to you. Do you remember the day when you asked me to be your wife? I was frank and open to you then, was I not?"

"You always are."

"I told you that if you wished it I would agree, but that I did not love you as a woman should love the man to whom she gives her life."

"I do not forget that."

"Perhaps in your heart you harboured a hope that one day the love that I denied you then might come?"

"I think I did."

"You were giving so much and asking for so little in return. That was not fair, and it would not be fair for me to allow you to harbour a hope that can never come true."

He turned slowly and looked at her.

"A woman cannot love—twice," she said slowly.

Johnny Everard flushed, then paled.

"Why do you say that?"

"Because it is true." She paused; the red dyed her cheeks. "What you were told last night were lies—poor lies. You do not ask me to deny them, dear, and so I won't. Yet, behind those lies, there was a little truth. There is a man, and I cared for him—care for him now and always shall care for him. He has been nothing to me, and never will be; but because he lived, because he and I have met, the hope that you had in your heart that day, can come to nothing. And now—now I have something more to tell you. It is this. You, who can love so finely, must ask for and have love in return. You think you love me, yet because I do not respond you will tire in time of that love. You will realise how bad a bargain you have made, and then you will regret it. Is there not someone"—her voice had grown low and soft—"someone who can and does give you all the love your heart craves for, someone who will be grateful to you for your love, and who will repay a thousandfold? Would not that be better than a long hopeless fight against lovelessness, even—even if you loved her a little less than you believe you love—me? Remember that it would rest with you and not with another, you who are generous, who could not refuse to give when so much is given to you." Joan's voice faltered for a moment. "It would be your own heart on which you would have to make the call, Johnny, not on the heart of another. You would have more command over your own heart than you ever could over the heart of another."

"Joan, what do you mean? What does this mean?"

"I am trying so hard to be plain," she said almost pitifully.

"Who is this other you are talking about, this other—who loves me?"

She was silent.

"What do you know of her, Joan, this other?"

And still she was silent, for how could she betray Ellice's secret?

"Tell me," he said.

"Don't you know? Can't you guess?"

His face flushed. A week ago he might have answered, "I cannot guess!" To-day he knew the answer, yet how did Joan know?

"I gave you my promise," she said, "and I will abide by that promise. It is for you to decide, and no one else. My life, your own and—and the life of another is in your hands—three futures, Johnny, decide—"

"You want to—to give me up?"

"Is that generous?"

"No, it isn't," he admitted. He took a turn up and down the room. "And you say this other—this girl—cares for me?"

"I know she does?"

"Did she tell you?"

"Must I answer?"

"Why not?"

"Why not?" Joan repeated. "Yes, she did. She came to me, openly and frankly, straightforward child that she is, and she said to me, 'Why are you marrying him, not loving him? If you loved him, and he loved you, I would not come to you; but you do not love him, and it is not fair. You are taking all and giving nothing!' And, she was right!"

"And she—she—" he said in a low voice, "would give—"

"Has given."

A silence fell between them. Then he turned to her, and it seemed as if the cloud had lifted from him. He held out his hands and smiled at her.

"I understand. You and she are right. A starved love could not live for ever; it must die. Better it should be strangled almost at birth, Joan. So—so this is good-bye?"

She shook her head. "Friends, always, Johnny," she said.

"Friends always, then."

She came close to him. She lifted her hand suddenly, and thrust back the hair from his forehead, she looked him in the eyes and, smiling, kissed him on the brow.

"Go and find your happiness—a far, far better than I could ever offer you."

"And you?"

She shook her head, and her eyes, looking beyond him into the garden, were dreamy and strangely soft.

"Tell me about that man, Johnny," she said. "Will you take me back to Little Langbourne with you?"

"Why?"

"To see him."

"But he maligned, he lied—"

"He is hurt, and why should I hate him? You did not believe. Will you take me back with you?"

"You know I will."

Helen, watching from the upper window, saw them drive away together, never had they seemed better friends. The cloud had passed completely away, and so too had all Helen's plans; yet she did not know it.

# CHAPTER XLVII

## "AS WE FORGIVE—"

Slotman opened dazed eyes and looked up into a face that might well have been the face of an angel, so soft, so pitying, so tender was its expression.

"Joan!" he whispered.

She nodded and smiled.

"But," he said—"but—" and hesitated. "Joan, I went to Buddesby to see—"

"I know."

"And yet you come here?"

"Of course. Hush! you must not talk. You are going to get well and strong again. The Matron says I am allowed to come sometimes and see you, and sit beside you, but you must not talk yet. Later on we are going to talk about the future."

He lay staring at her. He could not understand. How could such a mind as his understand the workings of such a mind as hers? But she was here, she knew and she forgave, and there was comfort in her presence.

God knew he had suffered. God knew it.

"When you are better, stronger, you and I are going to talk, not till then; but I want to tell you this now. I want to help you, all the past is past. I knew about that night, about your visit. It does not matter; it is all gone by. It is only the future that matters, and in the future you may find that I will give and help willingly what I would not have given under compulsion. Now, hush for the Matron is coming." She smiled down at him.

"I don't understand," Slotman said; "I'll try and understand." He turned his face away, realising a sense of shame such as he had never felt before.

He had been her enemy, and yet perhaps in his way, a bad and vile way, selfish and dishonourable, he had loved her; but as she had said, all that was of the past. Now she sat beside the man, broken in limb and in fortune, a wreck of what he had been; and for him her only feeling was of pity, and already in her mind she was forming plans for his future. For she had said truly she could give of her own free will and in charity and sympathy that which could never be forced from her.

Connie looked at her brother curiously.

\*   \*   \*   \*   \*

"I saw you just now. You drove past the gate with Joan. You took her to Langbourne, didn't you?"

"To the hospital. She went to see that fellow, Con."

"He told you something about Joan last night, Johnny?"

"He lied about the truest, purest woman who walks this earth."

"She is incapable of evil," Con said quietly.

"Utterly. Con, I have something to tell you."

She turned eagerly.

"It is ended," he said quietly—"our engagement. Joan and I ended it to-day—not in anger, not in doubt, dear, but liking and admiring each other I think more than ever before, and—and, Con—" He paused.

"Oh, I am glad, glad," she said, "glad! Have you told—her?"

He shook his head.

"Will you wait here, John? I will send her to you."

John Everard's face coloured. "I will wait here for her, for Gipsy," he said. "Send her here to me, and I will tell her, Con."

And a few moments later she came. She stood here in the doorway looking at him, just as she had looked at him from that same place that night, that night when a light had dawned upon his darkness.

And now, because his eyes were widely opened at last, he could see the tell-tale flush in her cheeks, the suspicious brightness in her eyes, and it seemed to him that her love for him was as a magnet that drew his heart towards her.

"Con has told you?"

She nodded silently.

Then suddenly he stretched out his arms to her, a moment more and she was in them, her face against his breast.

## CHAPTER XLVIII

## HER PRIDE'S LAST FIGHT

"... I came to Starden because I believed you might need me. You did, and the help that you wanted I gave gladly and willingly. Now your enemy is removed; he can do you no more harm. You will hear, or perhaps have heard why, and so I am no longer necessary to you, Joan, and because I seem to be wanted in my own place I am going back. Yet should you need me, you have but to call, and I will come. You know that. You know that I who love you am ever at your service. From now onward your own heart shall be your counsellor. You will act as it dictates, if you are true to yourself. Yet, perhaps in the future as in the past, your pride may prove the stronger. It is for you and only you to decide. Good-bye,

"HUGH."

She had found this letter on her return from Little Langbourne. She had gone hurrying, as a young girl in her eagerness might, down to Mrs. Bonner's little cottage, to learn that she was too late. He had gone.

Mrs. Bonner, with almost tears in her eyes, told her.

Henry St. John Cooper

"Yes, miss. He hev gone, and rare sorry I be, a better gentleman I never had in these rooms."

Gone! With only this letter, no parting word, without seeking to see her, to say good-bye. The chill of her cold pride fell on Joan. Send for him! Never! never! He had gone when he might have stayed—when, had he been here now, she would have told him that she was free.

Very slowly she walked back to the house, to meet Helen's questioning eyes.

"I am glad, dear, that there seems to be a better understanding between you and Johnny," Helen said.

"There is a perfect understanding between us. Johnny is not going to marry me. He is choosing someone who will love him more and understand him better than I could."

"Then—then, after all, it is over? You and he are to part?"

"Have parted—as lovers, but not as friends."

"And after all I have done," Helen said miserably.

Hugh had gone home. He had had a letter from Lady Linden telling about the accident to Tom Arundel, about his serious illness, and Marjorie's devoted nursing. And now he was shaping his course for Hurst Dormer. He had debated in his mind whether he should wait and see her, and then had decided against it.

"She knows that I love her, and she loves me. She is letting her pride stand between us. Everard is too good and too fine a fellow to keep her bound by a promise if he thought it would hurt her to keep it. Her future and Everard's and mine must lay in her own hands." And so, doing violence to his feelings and his desires, he had left Starden, and now was back in Hurst Dormer, wandering about, looking at the progress the workmen had made during his absence. He had come home, and though he loved the place, its loneliness weighed heavily on him. The rooms seemed empty. He wanted someone to talk things over with, to discuss this and that. He was not built to be self-centred.

For two days and two nights he bore with Hurst Dormer and its shadows and its solitude, and then he called out the car and motored over to Cornbridge.

"Oh, it's you," said her ladyship. "I suppose you got my letter?"

"Yes; I had it sent on to me."

"It's a pity you don't stay at home now and again."

"Perhaps I shall in future."

She looked at him. He was unlike himself, careworn and weary, and a little ill.

"Tom is mending rapidly, a wonderful constitution; but it was touch and go. Marjorie was simply wonderful, I'll do her that credit. Between ourselves, Hugh, I always regarded Marjorie as rather weak, namby-pamby, early Victorian— you know what I mean; but she's a woman, and it has touched her. She wouldn't leave him. Honestly, I believe she did more for him than all the doctors."

"I am sure she did."

Marjorie was changed; her face was thinner, some of its

colour gone. Yet the little she had lost was more than atoned for in the much that she had gained. She held his hand, she looked him frankly in the eyes.

"So it is all right, little girl, all right now?"

She nodded. "It is all right. I am happier than I deserve to be. Oh, Hugh, I have been weak and foolish, wavering and uncertain. I can see it all now, but now at last I know—I do know my own mind."

"And your own heart?"

"And my own heart."

She wondered as she looked at him if ever he could have guessed what had been in her mind that day when she had gone to Hurst Dormer to see him. How full of love for him her heart had been then! And then she remembered what he had said, those four words that had ended her dream for ever—"Better than my life." So he loved Joan, and now she knew that she too loved with her whole heart.

Death had been very close, and perhaps it had been pity for that fine young life that seemed to be so near its end that had awakened love. Yet, whatever the cause, she knew now that her love for Tom had come to stay.

"And Joan?" Marjorie asked.

"Joan?" he said. "Joan, she is in her own home."

"And her heart is still hard against you, Hugh?"

"Her pride is still between us, Marjorie," he said, and quickly turned the conversation, and a few minutes later was up in the bedroom talking cheerily enough to Tom.

"It's all right, Alston, everything is all right. Lady Linden wanted to shoot the horse; but I wouldn't have it. I owe him too much—you understand, Alston, don't you? Everything is all right between Marjorie and me."

And then Hugh went back to Hurst Dormer—thank, Heaven there was some happiness in this world! There was happiness at Cornbridge, and after Cornbridge Hurst Dormer seemed darker and more solitary than ever.

It was while she had been talking to Hugh that Marjorie had made up her mind.

"I am going to tell Joan the whole truth, the whole truth," she thought. And Hugh was scarcely out of the house before Marjorie sat down to write her letter to Joan.

"... I know that you have always blamed him for what was never his fault. He did it because he is generous and unselfish. He loved me in those days. I know that it could not have been the great abiding love; it was only liking that turned to fondness. Yet he wanted to marry me, Joan, and when he knew that there was someone else, and that he stood in the way of our happiness, the whole plan was arranged, and we had to find a name, you understand. And he asked me to suggest one, and I thought of yours, because it is the prettiest name I know; and he, Hugh, never dreamed that it belonged to a living woman. And so it was used, dear, and all this trouble and all this misunderstanding came about. I always wanted to tell you the truth, but he wouldn't let me, because he was afraid that if Aunt got to hear of it, she might be angry and send Tom away. But now I know she would not, and so I am telling you everything. The fault was mine. And yet, you know, dear, I had no thought of angering or of offending you. Write to me and tell me you forgive me. And oh, Joan, don't let pride come between you and the man you love, for I think he is one of the finest men I know, the best and straightest.

"MARJORIE."

Marjorie felt that she had lifted a weight from her mind when she put this letter in the post.

Long, long ago Joan had acquitted Hugh of any intention to offend or annoy her by the use of her name. Yet why had he never told her the truth, told her that it had never been his doing at all? She read Marjorie's letter, and then thrust it away from her. Why had he not written this? Did he care less now than he had? Had she tired him out with her coldness and her pride? Perhaps that was it.

Yesterday Ellice had come over on the old bicycle—Ellice with shining eyes and pink cheeks, glowing with happiness and joy, and Ellice had hugged her tightly, and tried to whisper thanks that would not come.

She was happy now. Marjorie was happy. Only she seemed to be cut off from happiness. Why had he gone without a word, just those few written lines? He had not cared so much, after all.

And so the days went by. Joan wrote a loving, sympathetic letter to Marjorie. She quite understood, and she did not blame Hugh; she blamed no one.

It was a long letter, dealing mainly with her life, with the village, with the things she was doing and going to do. But of the future—nothing; of the past, in so far as Hugh Alston was concerned—nothing.

And when Marjorie read the letter she read of an unsatisfied, unhappy spirit, of a girl whose whole heart yearned and longed for love, and whose pride held her in check and condemned her to unhappiness.

Scarcely a day passed but Joan drove over to Little Langbourne. Philip Slotman came to look for her, and counted it a long unhappy day if she failed him; but it was not often.

She had discovered that he was well-nigh penniless, and that it would be months before he would be fit to work again. And so she had quietly supplied all his needs.

"When you are well and strong again, you shall go back. You shall have the capital you want, and you will do well. I know that. I shall lend you the money to start afresh, and you will pay me back when you can."

"Joan, I wonder if there are many women like you?"

"Many better than I," she said—"many happier."

At Buddesby she was welcomed by a radiant girl with happy eyes, a girl who could not make enough of her, and there Joan saw a home life and happiness she had never known—a happiness that set her hungry heart yearning and longing with a longing that was intolerable and unbearable.

"Send for me, and I will come," he had written; and she had not sent. She would not, pride forbade it, and yet—yet to be happy as Ellice was happy, to feel his arms about her, to rest her head against his breast, to know that during all the years to come he would be here by her side, that loneliness would never touch her again.

"I won't!" she said. "I won't! If he needs me, it is he who must come to me. I will not send for him."

It was her pride's last fight, a fine fight it made. For days she struggled against the yearning of her heart, against the wealth of love, pent-up and stored within; valiantly and bravely pride fought.

To-day she had been to the hospital. She had stopped, as she often did, at Buddesby. There was talk of a marriage there. Many catalogues and price-lists had come through the post, and Con and Ellice were busy with them. For they were not very rich, and money must be made to go a long way; and into their conclave they drew Joan, who for a time forgot everything in this new interest.

They had all been very busy when the door had opened and Johnny Everard had come in, and, looking up, Joan caught a look that passed between Johnny and Ellice—just a look, yet it spoke volumes. It laid bare the secret of both hearts.

Later, when she said good-bye, he walked to the gate where her car was waiting. They had said but little, for Johnny seemed shy and constrained in her presence.

"Joan, I have much to be very, very grateful to you for," he said, as he held her hand. "You were right. Life without love would be impossible, and you have made life very possible for me."

She was thinking of this during the lonely drive back to Starden; always his words came back to her. Life without love would be impossible, and then it was that the battle ended, that pride retired vanquished from the field.

"I want you to come back to me because I am so lonely. Please come back and forgive.

"JOAN."

The message that, in the end, she must write was written and sent.

And now that pride had broken down, was gone for ever, so far as this man was concerned, it was a very loving anxious-eyed, trembling woman who watched for the coming of the man that she loved and needed, the man who meant all the happiness this world could give her.

\* \* \* \* \*

She had called to him, and this must be his answer. No slow-going trains, no tedious broken journeys, no wasted hours of delay—the fastest car, driven at reckless speed, yet with all due care that none should suffer because of his eagerness and his happiness.

It seemed to him such a very pitiful, humble little appeal, an appeal that went straight to his heart—so short an appeal that he could remember every word of it, and found himself repeating it as his car swallowed the miles that lay between them.

He asked no questions of himself. She would not have sent for him had she not been free to do so. He knew that.

And now the landscape was growing familiar, a little while, and they were running through Starden village. Villagers who had come to know him touched their hats. They passed Mrs. Bonner's little cottage, and now through the gateway, the gates standing wide as in welcome and expectation of his coming.

And she, watching for him, saw his coming, and her heart leaped with the joy of it. Helen Everard saw, too, and guessed what it meant.

"Go into the morning-room, Joan. I will send him to you there."

And so it was in the morning-room he found her. Flushed and bright-eyed, trembling with happiness and the joy of seeing him, gone for ever the pride and the scorn, she was only a girl who loved him dearly, who needed him much. She had fought the giant pride, and had beaten it for ever for his sake, and now he was here smiling at her, his arms stretched out to her.

"You wanted me at last, Joan," he said. "You called me, darling, and I have come."

"I want you. I always want you. Never, never leave me again, Hugh—never leave me again. I love you so, and need you so."

And then his arms were about her and hers about his neck, and she who had been so cold, so proud, so scornful, was remembering Johnny Everard's words, "Life without love would be impossible."

And now life was very, very possible to her.


THE END

# Choose from Thousands of 1stWorldLibrary Classics By

A. M. Barnard
Ada Leverson
Adolphus William Ward
Aesop
Agatha Christie
Alexander Aaronsohn
Alexander Kielland
Alexandre Dumas
Alfred Gatty
Alfred Ollivant
Alice Duer Miller
Alice Turner Curtis
Alice Dunbar
Allen Chapman
Alleyne Ireland
Ambrose Bierce
Amelia E. Barr
Amory H. Bradford
Andrew Lang
Andrew McFarland Davis
Andy Adams
Angela Brazil
Anna Alice Chapin
Anna Sewell
Annie Besant
Annie Hamilton Donnell
Annie Payson Call
Annie Roe Carr
Annonaymous
Anton Chekhov
Archibald Lee Fletcher
Arnold Bennett
Arthur C. Benson
Arthur Conan Doyle
Arthur M. Winfield
Arthur Ransome
Arthur Schnitzler
Arthur Train
Atticus
B.H. Baden-Powell
B. M. Bower
B. C. Chatterjee
Baroness Emmuska Orczy
Baroness Orczy
Basil King
Bayard Taylor
Ben Macomber
Bertha Muzzy Bower
Bjornstjerne Bjornson

Booth Tarkington
Boyd Cable
Bram Stoker
C. Collodi
C. E. Orr
C. M. Ingleby
Carolyn Wells
Catherine Parr Traill
Charles A. Eastman
Charles Amory Beach
Charles Dickens
Charles Dudley Warner
Charles Farrar Browne
Charles Ives
Charles Kingsley
Charles Klein
Charles Hanson Towne
Charles Lathrop Pack
Charles Romyn Dake
Charles Whibley
Charles Willing Beale
Charlotte M. Braeme
Charlotte M. Yonge
Charlotte Perkins Stetson
Clair W. Hayes
Clarence Day Jr.
Clarence E. Mulford
Clemence Housman
Confucius
Coningsby Dawson
Cornelis DeWitt Wilcox
Cyril Burleigh
D. H. Lawrence
Daniel Defoe
David Garnett
Dinah Craik
Don Carlos Janes
Donald Keyhoe
Dorothy Kilner
Dougan Clark
Douglas Fairbanks
E. Nesbit
E. P. Roe
E. Phillips Oppenheim
E. S. Brooks
Earl Barnes
Edgar Rice Burroughs
Edith Van Dyne
Edith Wharton

Edward Everett Hale
Edward J. O'Biren
Edward S. Ellis
Edwin L. Arnold
Eleanor Atkins
Eleanor Hallowell Abbott
Eliot Gregory
Elizabeth Gaskell
Elizabeth McCracken
Elizabeth Von Arnim
Ellem Key
Emerson Hough
Emilie F. Carlen
Emily Bronte
Emily Dickinson
Enid Bagnold
Enilor Macartney Lane
Erasmus W. Jones
Ernie Howard Pie
Ethel May Dell
Ethel Turner
Ethel Watts Mumford
Eugene Sue
Eugenie Foa
Eugene Wood
Eustace Hale Ball
Evelyn Everett-green
Everard Cotes
F. H. Cheley
F. J. Cross
F. Marion Crawford
Fannie E. Newberry
Federick Austin Ogg
Ferdinand Ossendowski
Fergus Hume
Florence A. Kilpatrick
Fremont B. Deering
Francis Bacon
Francis Darwin
Frances Hodgson Burnett
Frances Parkinson Keyes
Frank Gee Patchin
Frank Harris
Frank Jewett Mather
Frank L. Packard
Frank V. Webster
Frederic Stewart Isham
Frederick Trevor Hill
Frederick Winslow Taylor

| | | |
|---|---|---|
| Friedrich Kerst | Hayden Carruth | James Branch Cabell |
| Friedrich Nietzsche | Helent Hunt Jackson | James DeMille |
| Fyodor Dostoyevsky | Helen Nicolay | James Joyce |
| G.A. Henty | Hendrik Conscience | James Lane Allen |
| G.K. Chesterton | Hendy David Thoreau | James Lane Allen |
| Gabrielle E. Jackson | Henri Barbusse | James Oliver Curwood |
| Garrett P. Serviss | Henrik Ibsen | James Oppenheim |
| Gaston Leroux | Henry Adams | James Otis |
| George A. Warren | Henry Ford | James R. Driscoll |
| George Ade | Henry Frost | Jane Abbott |
| Geroge Bernard Shaw | Henry James | Jane Austen |
| George Cary Eggleston | Henry Jones Ford | Jane L. Stewart |
| George Durston | Henry Seton Merriman | Janet Aldridge |
| George Ebers | Henry W Longfellow | Jens Peter Jacobsen |
| George Eliot | Herbert A. Giles | Jerome K. Jerome |
| George Gissing | Herbert Carter | Jessie Graham Flower |
| George MacDonald | Herbert N. Casson | John Buchan |
| George Meredith | Herman Hesse | John Burroughs |
| George Orwell | Hildegard G. Frey | John Cournos |
| George Sylvester Viereck | Homer | John F. Kennedy |
| George Tucker | Honore De Balzac | John Gay |
| George W. Cable | Horace B. Day | John Glasgworthy |
| George Wharton James | Horace Walpole | John Habberton |
| Gertrude Atherton | Horatio Alger Jr. | John Joy Bell |
| Gordon Casserly | Howard Pyle | John Kendrick Bangs |
| Grace E. King | Howard R. Garis | John Milton |
| Grace Gallatin | Hugh Lofting | John Philip Sousa |
| Grace Greenwood | Hugh Walpole | John Taintor Foote |
| Grant Allen | Humphry Ward | Jonas Lauritz Idemil Lie |
| Guillermo A. Sherwell | Ian Maclaren | Jonathan Swift |
| Gulielma Zollinger | Inez Haynes Gillmore | Joseph A. Altsheler |
| Gustav Flaubert | Irving Bacheller | Joseph Carey |
| H. A. Cody | Isabel Cecilia Williams | Joseph Conrad |
| H. B. Irving | Isabel Hornibrook | Joseph E. Badger Jr |
| H. C. Bailey | Israel Abrahams | Joseph Hergesheimer |
| H. G. Wells | Ivan Turgenev | Joseph Jacobs |
| H. H. Munro | J. G.Austin | Jules Vernes |
| H. Irving Hancock | J. Henri Fabre | Julian Hawthrone |
| H. R. Naylor | J. M. Barrie | Julie A Lippmann |
| H. Rider Haggard | J. M. Walsh | Justin Huntly McCarthy |
| H. W. C. Davis | J. Macdonald Oxley | Kakuzo Okakura |
| Haldeman Julius | J. R. Miller | Karle Wilson Baker |
| Hall Caine | J. S. Fletcher | Kate Chopin |
| Hamilton Wright Mabie | J. S. Knowles | Kenneth Grahame |
| Hans Christian Andersen | J. Storer Clouston | Kenneth McGaffey |
| Harold Avery | J. W. Duffield | Kate Langley Bosher |
| Harold McGrath | Jack London | Kate Langley Bosher |
| Harriet Beecher Stowe | Jacob Abbott | Katherine Cecil Thurston |
| Harry Castlemon | James Allen | Katherine Stokes |
| Harry Coghill | James Andrews | L. A. Abbot |
| Harry Houidini | James Baldwin | L. T. Meade |

| | | |
|---|---|---|
| L. Frank Baum | Owen Johnson | Stephen Crane |
| Latta Griswold | P.G. Wodehouse | Stewart Edward White |
| Laura Dent Crane | Paul and Mabel Thorne | Stijn Streuvels |
| Laura Lee Hope | Paul G. Tomlinson | Swami Abhedananda |
| Laurence Housman | Paul Severing | Swami Parmananda |
| Lawrence Beasley | Percy Brebner | T. S. Ackland |
| Leo Tolstoy | Percy Keese Fitzhugh | T. S. Arthur |
| Leonid Andreyev | Peter B. Kyne | The Princess Der Ling |
| Lewis Carroll | Plato | Thomas A. Janvier |
| Lewis Sperry Chafer | Quincy Allen | Thomas A Kempis |
| Lilian Bell | R. Derby Holmes | Thomas Anderton |
| Lloyd Osbourne | R. L. Stevenson | Thomas Bailey Aldrich |
| Louis Hughes | R. S. Ball | Thomas Bulfinch |
| Louis Joseph Vance | Rabindranath Tagore | Thomas De Quincey |
| Louis Tracy | Rahul Alvares | Thomas Dixon |
| Louisa May Alcott | Ralph Bonehill | Thomas H. Huxley |
| Lucy Fitch Perkins | Ralph Henry Barbour | Thomas Hardy |
| Lucy Maud Montgomery | Ralph Victor | Thomas More |
| Luther Benson | Ralph Waldo Emmerson | Thornton W. Burgess |
| Lydia Miller Middleton | Rene Descartes | U. S. Grant |
| Lyndon Orr | Ray Cummings | Upton Sinclair |
| M. Corvus | Rex Beach | Valentine Williams |
| M. H. Adams | Rex E. Beach | Various Authors |
| Margaret E. Sangster | Richard Harding Davis | Vaughan Kester |
| Margret Howth | Richard Jefferies | Victor Appleton |
| Margaret Vandercook | Richard Le Gallienne | Victor G. Durham |
| Margaret W. Hungerford | Robert Barr | Victoria Cross |
| Margret Penrose | Robert Frost | Virginia Woolf |
| Maria Edgeworth | Robert Gordon Anderson | Wadsworth Camp |
| Maria Thompson Daviess | Robert L. Drake | Walter Camp |
| Mariano Azuela | Robert Lansing | Walter Scott |
| Marion Polk Angellotti | Robert Lynd | Washington Irving |
| Mark Overton | Robert Michael Ballantyne | Wilbur Lawton |
| Mark Twain | Robert W. Chambers | Wilkie Collins |
| Mary Austin | Rosa Nouchette Carey | Willa Cather |
| Mary Catherine Crowley | Rudyard Kipling | Willard F. Baker |
| Mary Cole | Saint Augustine | William Dean Howells |
| Mary Hastings Bradley | Samuel B. Allison | William le Queux |
| Mary Roberts Rinehart | Samuel Hopkins Adams | W. Makepeace Thackeray |
| Mary Rowlandson | Sarah Bernhardt | William W. Walter |
| M. Wollstonecraft Shelley | Sarah C. Hallowell | William Shakespeare |
| Maud Lindsay | Selma Lagerlof | Winston Churchill |
| Max Beerbohm | Sherwood Anderson | Yei Theodora Ozaki |
| Myra Kelly | Sigmund Freud | Yogi Ramacharaka |
| Nathaniel Hawthrone | Standish O'Grady | Young E. Allison |
| Nicolo Machiavelli | Stanley Weyman | Zane Grey |
| O. F. Walton | Stella Benson | |
| Oscar Wilde | Stella M. Francis | |